How to Use Your Rea
in Your Essays

www.skills4study.com – the leading study skills website with FREE study tips, downloads and advice

Palgrave Study Guides

Authoring a PhD
Business Degree Success
Career Skills
Critical Thinking Skills
e-Learning Skills (2nd edn)
Effective Communication for
    Arts and Humanities Students
Effective Communication for
    Science and Technology
The Exam Skills Handbook
The Foundations of Research
The Good Supervisor
Great Ways to Learn Anatomy and Physiology
How to Manage your Arts, Humanities and
    Social Science Degree
How to Manage your Distance and
    Open Learning Course
How to Manage your Postgraduate Course
How to Manage your Science and
    Technology Degree
How to Study Foreign Languages
How to Use Your Reading in Your Essays
How to Write Better Essays (2nd edn)
How to Write your Undergraduate Dissertation
IT Skills for Successful Study
The International Student Handbook
Making Sense of Statistics
The Mature Student's Handbook
The Mature Student's Guide to Writing (2nd edn)
The Personal Tutor's Handbook

The Postgraduate Research Handbook (2nd edn)
Presentation Skills for Students
The Principles of Writing in Psychology
Professional Writing (2nd edn)
Researching Online
Research Using IT
Skills for Success
The Study Abroad Handbook
The Student's Guide to Writing (2nd edn)
The Student Life Handbook
The Study Skills Handbook (3rd edn)
Study Skills for International Postgraduates
Study Skills for Speakers of English as a
    a Second Language
Studying the Built Environment
Studying Business at MBA and Masters Level
Studying Economics
Studying History (3rd edn)
Studying Law (2nd edn)
Studying Mathematics and its Applications
Studying Modern Drama (2nd edn)
Studying Physics
Studying Programming
Studying Psychology (2nd edn)
Teaching Study Skills and Supporting Learning
Work Placements – a Survival Guide for Students
Writing for Nursing and Midwifery Students
Write it Right
Writing for Engineers (3rd edn)

Palgrave Study Guides: Literature

General Editors: John Peck and Martin Coyle

How to Begin Studying English Literature
    (3rd edn)
How to Study a Jane Austen Novel (2nd edn)
How to Study a Charles Dickens Novel
How to Study Chaucer (2nd edn)
How to Study an E. M. Forster Novel
How to Study James Joyce
How to Study Linguistics (2nd edn)

How to Study Modern Poetry
How to Study a Novel (2nd edn)
How to Study a Poet
How to Study a Renaissance Play
How to Study Romantic Poetry (2nd edn)
How to Study a Shakespeare Play (2nd edn)
How to Study Television
Practical Criticism

How to Use Your Reading in Your Essays

Jeanne Godfrey

palgrave
macmillan

First published 2009 by
PALGRAVE MACMILLAN

Palgrave Macmillan in the UK is an imprint of Macmillan Publishers Limited,
registered in England, company number 785998, of Houndmills, Basingstoke,
Hampshire RG21 6XS.

Palgrave Macmillan in the US is a division of St Martin's Press LLC,
175 Fifth Avenue, New York, NY 10010.

Palgrave Macmillan is the global academic imprint of the above companies
and has companies and representatives throughout the world.

Palgrave® and Macmillan® are registered trademarks in the United States,
the United Kingdom, Europe and other countries.

ISBN-13: 978-0230-20540-6   paperback
ISBN-10: 0230-20540-2   paperback

This book is printed on paper suitable for recycling and made from fully
managed and sustained forest sources. Logging, pulping and manufacturing
processes are expected to conform to the environmental regulations of the
country of origin.

A catalogue record for this book is available from the British Library.

A catalog record for this book is available from the Library of Congress.

10 9 8 7 6 5 4 3 2 1
18 17 16 15 14 13 12 11 10 09

Printed in China

For my mother, Patricia

Contents

Appendices   107

Acknowledgements

This book is a product of my learning and experience gained over the years from the students I have taught, colleagues I have worked with, and writers and experts in the field – my thanks to them all. I also thank the writers in other disciplines whose work I have used and acknowledge in this book. I am extremely grateful to the reviewers of early versions of the typescript for taking the time to go through them, and for their important and useful comments. I would also like to thank the staff at Palgrave Macmillan for guiding me through the writing process so smoothly, particularly Suzannah Burywood for being encouraging and helpful from the start, and Jocelyn Stockley for finding my many mistakes in both sense and form.

Finally, I would like to thank my husband Chris for all his support and encouragement.

Note

The website www.palgrave.com/studyskills/godfrey situates this book within further and higher education, gives tutors and lecturers some suggestions for using it with students, and suggests further ways of developing students' writing. I would welcome comments and feedback on this book which can be emailed to godfreyfeedback@palgrave.com.

Introduction

● **What this book gives you**

A fundamental part of academic study is reading other people's work on a subject and using what you have read in your own thinking and writing. This ability is also a key communication skill which employers look for in graduates. This book will take you through the process for doing this, from deciding what to read to checking your work for mistakes. It looks at using your reading for writing essays, but the information it gives is relevant to all types of academic writing across all subject areas. This book will give you the knowledge, practice and confidence you need, to use your reading effectively to produce good writing and to get the highest marks possible for your work.

This book will show you:

- how to decide which types of books and articles are suitable to read for your essays and which are probably not;
- how to understand and question what you read;
- what information to write down and how to make notes which enable you to use your reading properly and effectively in your essays;
- why, when and how to use quotations in your essays;
- why, when and how to put what you read into your own words;
- why, when and how to put together your own points with ideas from your reading;
- key words and phrases you will need to use when you are using your reading in your essays;
- common grammatical mistakes to look for when you are checking your essays.

This book will take you through these stages by giving you key points of information, highlighting common problems and giving you examples and practice from real texts and student essays. It explains simply and clearly both the 'why' of using your reading and the practical 'how' for doing so, and tells you what words such as *research*, *literature search*, *research log*, *critical analysis*, *literature review* and *plagiarism* mean.

The rest of this introductory section gives you a useful overview of how reading is used in an essay and key points to remember when you are writing your essays.

● Overview of using sources

An example of how reading is used in an essay

Below are two sections (introduction and middle) of a good student essay. At university you will be given different types of coursework assignments on a variety of topics, but the style of writing in this essay will be common to most of them. We will look at different sections of this essay throughout this book and the complete essay is given on pages 115–18.

Look at the essay sections and notice how the student has used the books and articles he has read (these are called sources) in his essay. The essay sections are colour-coded to help you do this.

Black = **student** – student's own knowledge, ideas and words

Blue = **source** – information and ideas from what the student has read, using either the exact words from the source (a quotation) or his own words (a paraphrase or summary)

Red = **in-essay reference** – information which indicates when a source has been used and who the author is

Outline what business ethics is and discuss whether it is important. (1,500 words)

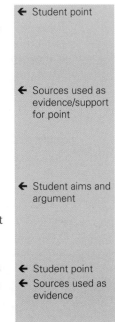

The subject of business ethics has become increasingly important over the past few decades and now appears to be a prevalent factor in consumer choice. An illustration of this is the current number of publications in the UK which give consumers information on so-called ethical companies. The Ethical Company Organisation (2008), for example, lists businesses ranging from pet food producers and florists, to banks and stationery companies. The UK ethical market is valued at over 40 billion euros per year and there are currently over 2,000 books and 4 million web entries related to business ethics (Crane and Matten, 2007). This essay will first describe what business ethics is and secondly, will consider whether this concept really is important. It will argue that business ethics is indeed a real and major issue in both the study and practice of business.

There are numerous but similar definitions of business ethics given by academic experts. Shaw and Barry (2007) define business ethics as 'the study of what constitutes right and wrong (or good and bad) human conduct in a

← Student point

← Sources used as evidence/support for point

← Student aims and argument

← Student point
← Sources used as evidence

business context' (p. 25). Another definition describes business ethics as the 'principles and standards that guide behaviour in the world of business' (Ferrell and Fraedrich et al., 2002, p. 6). A growing number of companies also have their own descriptions of what they understand by ethical behaviour. Many companies list only the quality, naturalness and sustainability of their products as their underlying ethical message. One example of a company statement which also includes the human dimension is the following: 'we will operate our business with a strong commitment to the well being of our fellow humans and the preservation of the planet' (Body Shop International, Policy on donations, May 2006, p. 1).

← Student point

← Source used as support

. . .

There are diverse opinions as to whether ethics do have a valid place in a business. These views range from a definite 'no' i.e. that ethics does not and should not play a part in business, to a clear 'yes' and the argument that ethical behaviour should be a core value in any organisation. Opponents of the concept of ethics in business include those who claim that making a profit is the only responsibility a business has to society (Friedman, 1970, cited in Fisher and Lovell, 2003). Others such as Wolf (2008) share this view, and Prindl and Prodham (1994) suggest that 'Finance as practised in the professions and in industry is seen as a value-neutral positive discipline promoting efficiency without regard to the social consequences which follow from its products' (p. 3). Carr (1968) uses the analogy of a poker game to argue that a successful businessman needs to play by the rules of business, in which 'bluffing' is an acceptable form of behaviour, and that these rules are distinct from personal or social values. He suggests that even if a manager claims that good ethical conduct is also good for business, s/he is not really making a choice to be ethical but is merely using ethical conduct as a profitable business strategy.

← Student point

← Sources used as evidence and support

It is of course true that most businesses cannot succeed without being profitable. However, this does not necessarily exclude ethical behaviour and although Carr's view seems persuasive, there are two strong opposing arguments which are even more so.

← Student point

. . .

● **Comments on how the student has used his reading in his essay**

The student's own points (shown in black)

The essay sections show five main points that the student has made as part of his whole argument. Each time the student introduces his own point, he uses what he has read (his sources) as evidence or support for the point he is making. He then usually gives a final comment of his own and then moves on to his next point.

Use of sources (shown in blue)

Note that the student has used only four short quotations (indicated by quotation marks '. . .') and two of these are definitions. His complete essay uses a total of only six short quotations; most of the time the student has put the sources into his own words.

Use of in-essay references (shown in red)

Every time the student uses a source he gives it an in-essay reference (sometimes called an in-text reference or citation). He does this not only when he has used quotations, but also when he has put a source into his own words. These references make clear to the reader which ideas or comments are his own and which ones come from his reading.

The student has used the author/year system for his in-essay references and this system will be used throughout this book. The other main way of referencing is to use a sequence of numbers and corresponding footnotes, called the numeric system. Examples of the numeric system are given in the answers to exercises in sections A4 and A5 and a brief summary of different referencing styles is given in Appendix 4, on page 113.

Five key points to remember when you are writing an essay

1 **Preparing and writing an essay at university involves three main processes:**

   ● reading the work of others to develop your own knowledge and thoughts on a subject;
   ● using what you have read to develop your own argument and answer to the essay title;
   ● expressing and explaining what you have read, in your own words, as part of your own argument.

2 **Don't be afraid of using sources and showing that you have used them.**
   Your tutors will usually want your essay to use sources quite a lot and will expect you to use in-essay references. This is so that they can see

what you have read and how you have used other people's ideas to develop your own argument and apply your knowledge to the essay question. Your essay will still be original to you because of the choices you have made in selecting which sources to use, how you have put the ideas into your own words and how you have used them to answer your essay title.

3   Every time you use words and/or ideas from your reading, use an in-essay reference.

If you only give in-essay references for some of your sources but not all of them, your tutor will not be able to see which parts of the essay are your *own* points and so you may not get the marks you deserve for these. At first you might feel that putting in a reference each time you use a source results in too many references in your essay but using references is good scholarship and you will get marks for this. Another important reason for always giving references is to avoid accidentally representing ideas from your reading as your own.

4   Put your reading into your own words as much as possible.

Using your own words shows that you have understood what you have read and allows you to rework, control and use your reading to support your own points. It helps you to develop your own thoughts and ideas and to get good marks. Re-interpreting information in your own words is also central to the good written communication skills that employers look for in graduates.

5   Using your reading properly in your own writing takes time and practice.

Even professional writers can find writing very difficult. Good writing takes time and practice, and integrating your reading into your own writing is a very complex skill. Your tutors will expect you to develop these writing skills gradually and will not want to read essays that try to be over-complicated or are full of long words. They want to see writing that is clear and well thought out and the key to this is to give enough time to all three parts of the writing process: reading, thinking and writing.

Part A Using your reading

Introduction to Part A: Key points for reading

The types of books and articles you read at university will probably be different from those you used at school and college. Why and how you read at university will also be different, requiring more independence from you in deciding what to read, higher levels of concentration and more questioning of the material. Finally, as you will have seen from the main introduction, the way in which reading is used in academic essays makes this type of writing quite different from work you may have done up to now.

What Part A gives you

- Key points and strategies to take you through the process of reading and using your reading in your essays.
- Real academic articles, real student writing and a short student essay to demonstrate each stage of the process.
- Short exercises for you to check and practise your understanding.

It is best to go through each section of Part A in order but you can of course also read and re-read different sections as and when you need them.

Five key points to remember about reading

- A common reason why students struggle with reading at university is simply that they do not give enough time to it. Think seriously about this and make reading a priority in your time management schedule.

- Identify your purpose for reading a book or article and decide what it is you want to learn from it. Then be flexible in how you read, so that the way you go about it matches your purpose for reading. For example, you may need to read one article from start to finish but for another you may only need to read one particular paragraph.

- Try to engage with the material rather than just reading the words on the page. This means being (or becoming) interested in what you are reading, and thinking about what the author is doing and trying to say. This will greatly improve your understanding and will further increase your interest in the subject.

- The books and articles you will be asked to read may seem complex, formal and difficult to understand at first. Everyone approaches reading in a slightly different way and it may take a little time to build up your 'reading muscles' and to discover what works best for you. Start by reading short sections before tackling longer ones. As with everything else, you will improve with practice.

- Reading will also help improve your writing skills, by increasing your knowledge of new words and your awareness of how to structure a piece of written work. Bear in mind, however, that not everything you read will be well written.

A1 How do you decide what to read?

It seems obvious that for a good essay you need good sources but what exactly *is* a 'good' source? When looking for sources, don't be tempted to just type your essay title straight into a general search engine in the hope that something useful will come up. Knowing what types of sources are suitable for university work and spending some time thinking about what information you need, will save you a great deal of time and will result in a much better piece of work. This section gives you the key steps and information you need for finding the best sources for your essay.

● Five key steps for deciding what to read

Step 1   Think: what question do you want to answer?
Do some thinking before you start searching for sources. Check that you really understand the title of your essay. For example, does the title ask you to develop an argument, give your opinion, give examples, or some of these things together? Does it ask for definitions, information on a process, advantages and disadvantages, or for different views on an issue?

Rewrite the title in your own words as this will really help you to understand it. For example, the business ethics essay title could be rewritten as: 'Give a brief description of what business ethics is and then argue that business ethics either is or is not important, giving your reasons for your view.'

Step 2   Think: what ideas of your own do you already have?
You will probably already have done some reading and discussion on the essay topic during your course, so think about what you have read that is relevant to the essay title and what your own thoughts are on the essay question. For the business ethics essay, you would ask yourself what *you* think business ethics is and whether *you* think it is important.

Step 3   Think: what *types* of source will you need?
Make notes on any suggested reading and other instructions about sources your tutor has given you and think about what types of sources you will need, to answer your essay title.

For example, which of the following will you need?

- An introductory textbook to give you some initial ideas;
- chapters in more advanced textbooks;
- important major works on the topic;
- original data from experiments or other research;
- recent academic journal articles on new developments or ideas on the topic;
- non-expert or public opinion on an issue.

For the business ethics essay, the student decided to look in some current academic textbooks for definitions of business ethics. He also read some relevant journal articles by key authors for their views on the importance of business ethics, and he decided to look at some company websites to find out what businesses themselves say about business ethics.

Step 4   Do a first search

First, you need to decide how good you want your essay to be and how much time and effort you are willing to give to finding the right sources for it. Then use the notes you have made on the types of sources you need, and start searching. Searching for sources is called a 'literature search' and it is the start of your own academic research. As you search, keep checking that your sources are relevant, specific and reliable.

Content pages and chapter headings of books, and journal article abstracts, can help you to decide whether a source is relevant. Reading the introduction and conclusion of a book chapter or journal article is also a quick way of finding out whether a source will be useful. The reference list at the end of one book or article may provide you with details of further useful sources.

Remember however, that abstracts, summaries and reviews are useful for a first search but are not acceptable as sources for your essay; you will need to read the full article or book section. Similarly, basic introductory and/or college-level books or encyclopaedias may be useful to get some initial ideas but are not good enough as a source for a university-level essay.

It is important at this stage to write down the precise details of each source (name, date, title, publisher etc.) and also where and how you found it, in case you need to find it again at a later stage in your research. You may not think that it is important to do this but you will be surprised how useful this information is – and remember that for academic work, *who* wrote something is as important as what they wrote about.

Step 5   Think, sort and select your sources for detailed reading

When you have done your first search for sources, think again about what you will want to say in your essay and what you think your conclusion will be. This may change as you read more, but by now you should have some idea of how you want to answer the essay title.

You might need to do some general background reading on a topic but most essay titles will ask for something specific. Try not to waste time reading sources which may be on the correct general topic but which are not specific enough. For example, for the business ethics essay you would not want to spend time reading about general business topics or about the meaning or history of ethics. You would need to focus specifically on *business* ethics. Even when you had found a book on business ethics, you would not need to read it all, just the chapters or sections which described what business ethics is, whether it is important, and why.

Select your sources for more detailed reading and ask yourself the following questions about each source.

- What type of source is it and who wrote it?
- Is it relevant and specific to my essay?
- Is it a reliable and academic source?
- Why am I going to read it?
- Will it probably support my conclusion or give an opposing viewpoint?
- Will I probably use it as an important piece of information or only as a minor source?

● What is a reliable source?

At university you are expected to make sure that your sources are reliable – that you can trust what they say. This usually means knowing who wrote something and that they are an authority on their topic. Reliable sources are generally those that have a named author as this ensures that readers know who is responsible and accountable for the information given. Anonymous sources are much more likely to be of poor quality and/or contain incorrect information.

Up-to-date information will probably be more reliable than older information, so check when your source was written. You may want to read older sources because they are important texts and to build up your knowledge, but for most topics you will also need current sources. Always check online sources to see when they were last updated and whether any links are active.

A reliable source is also one that gives information which is as accurate and complete as possible, rather than giving only the information which suits a particular purpose (called bias). Business and political organisations, for example, may present information in a biased way. However, bear in mind what 'reliable' means for the type of information you need. If your essay is about public opinion in the media, then newspapers and television programmes would be a reliable source for this particular type of information. Equally, if you are writing about the views of different political organisations, then the leaflets and websites of these organisations would provide reliable information on what these views are, even though such information may not be balanced or reliable in the general sense of the word.

● Primary and secondary sources

You should try to find the original (primary) source of information where possible, as something that is reported second or third hand may not be accurate and will be less reliable. If you want data on the results of an experiment, try to read the original report rather than a later article that discusses the experiment and data (this is called a secondary source). Similarly, if you want to write about what an expert has said, read the actual book or article they have written, rather than an article by another author who discusses what the expert has said. In reality, it will not always be possible or necessary to use only primary sources, but be aware that you will usually be expected to read the key primary sources on a topic.

For the business ethics essay, the student found some primary material about companies from their websites. The textbooks and articles he used were partly primary material but these sources also discussed the previous work of other experts and so acted as secondary sources of the primary material they mentioned. Several of the articles the student read refrred to an important text written by Albert Carr in 1968, so the student made sure that he found and read this primary source.

● What is an academic source?

For most assignments at university, you will need to use information from sources which are not only reliable but are also regarded as academic. Academic sources are those written by experts (or authorities) on a topic and which have been peer-reviewed. The peer-review process is when the book or article is sent by the publisher to other experts for checking and discussion before being published. Peer-reviewed sources are reliable and are called 'academic' (or 'reputable' or 'authoritative') sources because they have been written by people who have attained a high standard of knowledge and research in their subject. Reliable and academic sources always have a named author or organisation. The academic community relies on knowing who wrote what, so that academics in a particular field of study can question, discuss and work with each other to build knowledge and develop ideas.

● Non-academic sources

Below is a list of source types which are not academic and should not normally be used as sources for essays:

- newspapers (including long articles in quality papers such as *The Times* or the *Guardian*);
- magazines (including quality magazines such as *The Economist*, *Newsweek* and *New Scientist*);
- news or TV channel websites (e.g. the *BBC News*);
- trade publications and company websites;
- publications and websites of charities, campaign or pressure groups;

- student theses or essays;
- Wikipedia;
- pamphlets and brochures;
- blogs and wikis.

Checking that your sources are academic

Books and journals on the library shelves and on your reading lists will usually be reliable and academic. However, you may want to find other sources and you will need to make the effort to check that these are also reliable and academic. Books have normally gone through a peer-review process and so are usually reliable. Journals described as an academic journal, a peer-reviewed journal or a scholarly journal will be reliable and academic.

Check your online sources

Take particular care when you are using online sources. Your tutor will suggest suitable places to search online but it is your responsibility to check that your sources are reliable and academic. Wikipedia may be useful for some initial definitions and to give you links to other sources but you should not use it as an actual source in your essay. This is because Wikipedia is a type of encyclopaedia and is therefore only a basic summary and a secondary source. It is also anonymous and is not peer-reviewed and is therefore not reliable and not academic.

Words that should warn you that an online article is probably not academic are: *magazine, digest, news, press release, correspondent, journalist, special report company, classified, personals* and *advertisement*. Don't be fooled into thinking that an online article is reliable and academic just because it is well written and has an author's name, statistics and in-text references. Even words such as *journal, research, volume/issue number, Society* or *Research Centre* are being increasingly used by unreliable and non-academic sources and websites. You need to check that the article is in fact from a peer-reviewed journal.

Check your online databases

Some online databases contain only peer-reviewed academic journals but some of them (even some which describe themselves as a 'research database') also contain newspapers, magazines and trade publications. Read the description of the database before you go into it; what does it say it contains? You may be able to google a database and get a description of its publications from the 'home' or 'about us' page. Remember – always check whether an article is academically reliable even if you have found it through a database.

Check your web search engines

Search engines such as Google, Wanadoo and Yahoo are not good places to look for academic sources. Google Scholar is useful as it finds only scholarly literature but you still need to be careful, as not all of this literature is peer-reviewed material – it also includes some magazines and student theses.

●   Where to check a website

If you are not sure about the reliability of an online website, article, database or search engine, try to find its homepage and look under sections such as 'about us', 'contact us', 'editorial board', 'board of directors', 'information for authors', 'submission process', 'sponsors', 'funders' and 'partners'.

These sections will give you information about who runs and supports the site and whether its articles are peer-reviewed.

Practice 1: Would you use these sources?

Read the descriptions below of ten potential sources for five different essay titles. Do you think these sources are 'not reliable', 'reliable but not academic' or 'reliable *and* academic'?

Sources for an essay on government support for people with disabilities

1   An article written in July 2006 in an online magazine called 'Mobility Now'. It has news, information and stories and is a magazine for people with disabilities. It is published by a leading charity organisation for people with disabilities.

Sources for an essay on youth crime

2   A recent online article on ASBOs written by Jane Smith, Home Correspondent. The URL is the online business section of a national quality newspaper.

Sources for an essay on recent developments in stem cell research

3   An online article on stem cells, published jointly by three authors in 2002. The article has a date, volume and issue number. The article appears on a website called 'Stem Cells'. This seems to be the title of the journal and at the bottom of the page there is a publisher: Beta Res Press. In the 'information for authors' section, the website tells authors how to track the progress of their article as it goes through the peer-review process.

4   Three different online science publications with similar titles, which all look like magazines. They all have news sections, advertise-

ments and jobs sections. They all have issue numbers and two of them also have volume numbers.

4a   The first one has an 'about us' page which describes how its correspondents get their information by contacting leading scientists, reading scientific journals and websites, and attending conferences.

4b   The second magazine has the name of an organisation at the top of its website. On its 'about' page it describes the magazine as its journal and states that it is a peer-reviewed general science journal. When you read another page you find that the members of its board of directors are all university academics.

4c   The third publication has no 'about us' information, so you enter the magazine title on Wikipedia. Wikipedia describes the magazine as 'a well-respected publication despite not being peer-reviewed'.

Sources for an essay on recent developments in animal cloning

5.   An article from a printed booklet titled 'Animal Cloning' published in 1999. There is a series of booklets, each with a volume and issue number. Each booklet contains a collection of short articles and newspaper and magazine clippings which give a simple introduction to issues and public debate on a scientific topic.

Sources for an essay on business ethics

6   A well-written report (which starts with an executive summary) on business ethics in companies. The website is run by an organisation called SEB – Social Ethics in Business. On the 'about us' page, the organisation describes itself as part of a network of business organisations that focus on corporate responsibility. Its funders and partners are large national and international business foundations and development agencies.

7   An online article titled 'Business Ethics Guidelines'. The website address is 'Harold Jones International Company'.

8   An online article about McDonald's on a website called 'Centre for Management Research'. There is no 'about us' page but there is a homepage which states that the centre is involved in business research, management consulting and the development of case studies and training materials.

9   An online article on business ethics found on the website of the 'Centre for Business Ethics' of a university. On the centre's home-page it states that the centre helps businesses and the community and offers workshops, conferences and lectures. It also states that the centre publishes its own 'Journal of Ethics'.

10 An online article about a drinks company's activities in India. The article has no author but is well written and says 'for immediate release' at the top of the page. The website is titled as a 'Resource Centre'. The 'home/about' page states that the centre has grown out of networks and discussions by activists, and describes itself as a platform for movements to publicise demands and to put pressure on governments.

(The articles and websites are fictitious but are closely based on real examples.)

A2 How do you understand and question what you read?

When you sit down to read a book, chapter or article (we can call all of these 'texts') you should usually already know what type of text it is, who wrote it, that it is reliable and academic and that it is relevant and specific to your essay question. You will probably also have some idea of what it is about and why you are going to read it. You may think then that actually reading the text would be quite straightforward. However, one of the most common reasons why students get low marks for their essays is that they have not read carefully enough or not properly understood the main points of the text. To use your sources effectively you need to really understand each text and to read it with some questions in mind. This section gives you steps, examples and practice for doing this.

● Three key steps to understanding and questioning what you read

Step 1 Think: what questions will you have in mind as you read?
Before you start reading a text, decide what type of information you are looking for. For example:

- Are you looking for the answers to specific questions (for example, what business ethics is or whether it is important)?
- Are you looking for general information on a point that you don't know much about and that will help you develop your own ideas and argument?
- Are you just looking for a few basic facts or do you need to read in detail so that you can follow the author's argument?
- Are you looking for evidence and examples as support for what you want to argue in your essay?
- Are you looking for points that you will then argue against?

Step 2 Read and think
Read with your questions in mind. If you are only looking for one or two facts, you can just quickly scan the text for this information. Usually however, you will want to read in more detail.

It may be better *not* to write anything down at this stage. Read the first section of the text (or all of a short text) and just try to understand:

- what the main point of the text is;
- which parts of the text are main points, which are more minor points and which parts of the text are examples of points made;
- which parts of the text are facts or description and which are the author's opinion.

Try to identify what the author is trying to do. For example, are they giving information, putting forward an idea or theory, arguing and trying to persuade you of something, or a combination of these things?

Then try to explain to yourself what the main point of the text is, in your own words.

Step 3   Read and ask questions

Read the text again and this time, question, evaluate and locate what the author says, using the prompts below (you can do this either in your head or on paper).

Questioning what the author says
- What assumptions does the author make?
- Do you think these assumptions are correct?
- Are the stages of the argument clear and logical?
- Does the conclusion follow from the evidence given?

Evaluating what the author says
- Are you persuaded by what the author says? Why/why not?
- If someone asked your opinion of the author's viewpoint, what would you say?
- How will you use what the author says in *your* argument?

Locating the author in the subject area
- What is the author's position on the issue?
- How does the author's argument and position fit in with what you already know?
- How is the author's argument different from or similar to those of other experts on this subject?
- Does the author's argument belong to a particular school of thought (e.g. behaviourism, Marxism, feminism)?

● Opinion, critical analysis and argument

Students often think (or are told) that they should not give their opinions in an essay. It is true that you should not just give your personal opinion about something based only on your feelings. However, you *are* expected to give your opinion on an issue or essay question, provided that you have arrived at this opinion through clear reasoning.

Your reasons should be supported by evidence and you should come to a conclusion which is persuasive because it follows logically from your reasoning and evidence. This sequence is called an argument. 'Arguing' in academic study does not mean that you have to argue *against* something; an argument in the academic sense means a logical, structured and evidenced response to an issue or question.

As part of your argument, you will need to state whether you agree or disagree with the sources you discuss and you won't be able to do this unless you have questioned, evaluated and located them, as shown above. This thought process is called *critical thinking* or *critical analysis*. As with the word *argument*, *critical thinking* in the academic sense does not mean that you can only say negative things about a text; indeed, you might want to be very positive about something you read. Critically analysing a text just means that you have asked yourself questions about what it says and formed your own views on it, based on clear reasoning rather than just your personal experience or opinion.

● Looking at an example of questioning, evaluating and locating a text

Below are three short sections from a long article which the student read for his business ethics essay. Read the extracts to give you some idea of the authors' arguments and then look at the informal notes, which show the student's thoughts when he questioned, evaluated and located the whole article.

A Model of Business Ethics

If one searches the literature, it appears that in the thirty years that business ethics has been a discipline in its own right a model of business ethics has not been proffered. This paper attempts to address this gap in the literature by proposing a model of business ethics that the authors hope will stimulate debate. . . . This model is one that is predicated on the tenets of developed countries operating within a capitalist paradigm.

. . .

Socially responsible managers do the right thing because it is the right thing to do. It is the correct action to take and an action that society expects. Executives should 'act ethically not out of fear of being caught when doing wrong. Rather, they should embrace ethical behaviour in business because of the freedom, self-confirmation, and success that it brings' (Thomas et al., 2004, p. 64).

. . . it is important to see business ethics as a highly dynamic and continuous process without an end. A process, however, that is predicated on the interrelationship between business and society where each one is interdependent and responsible together for the outcomes. Hoffman and Moore (1982) suggest that the pre-eminence of business ethics is because of a perceived failing, by the general community, of business to act for the general good of the society. They, therefore, suggest that the mutual obligations of business to the community and the community to business need to be restated.

(Extracts from: Svensson, G. and Wood, G. (2008) 'A Model of Business Ethics'. *Journal of Business Ethics*, 77, pp. 303–22.)

The student's thoughts on the text

Questioning

The authors look at businesses operating in a developed world, capitalist context. Presumably there are lots of businesses outside this type of context – how do they behave? Svensson and Wood also seem to assume that individuals and society always expect businesses to behave well, and that people trust businesses – I don't think they do. They also assume that there are socially responsible managers who want to do what is right – this might not be a correct assumption and they don't give any examples as evidence of this.

Evaluating

It's a good persuasive argument – seems to be well researched and expert. The article is very clear and well-structured and has detailed points. Their conclusion is supported by evidence, although this is mainly by reference to other authors – I will need to read a couple of these primary sources for myself.

Svensson and Wood argue strongly and clearly that business and society influence each other and are dependent on each other and have a responsibility to each other to behave ethically. However, they seem to ignore the fact that not everyone thinks we should trust businesses or that organisations should be responsible to society and their argument seems to be based on some unproven assumptions. Also, Svensson and Wood leave out some other simple models of business ethics I've read about and they don't use real business examples for some of their points – they only make references to primary sources which have examples.

Still, I think that this article is solid enough to use as one of my main sources as evidence for what I think my conclusion will probably be, which is that business ethics is important both to businesses and to society.

Locating

The article puts forward a theoretical model which they say has not been done before and that it is therefore doing something new, filling a gap in theory. They probably expect other academics to argue or disagree with their model of business ethics.

Their argument fits in with what I think. Svensson and Wood agree with other articles I have read by Esty, Collins, Shaw and Barry and these are all on the opposite side to Freidman, Wolf and Carr. I think that this article is an important one on the issue I think, because it is very recent and seems to bring together in a detailed and persuasive way what a lot of the other articles from the last 10 years have said.

Practice 2: How would you question, evaluate and locate this article?

Below are sections from another article (the 1968 article by Albert Carr) which the student used for his business ethics essay. Read the sections and then briefly question, evaluate and locate them. You should be able to do this without any specific business knowledge.

There is not one correct answer to this exercise but you can compare your thoughts with those on pages 122–123.

Is business bluffing ethical?

We can learn a good deal about the nature of business by comparing it with poker. Poker's own brand of ethics is different from the ethical ideals of civilized human relationships as the game calls for distrust of the other fellow. . . .

That most businessmen are not indifferent to ethics in their private lives, everyone will agree. My point is that in their office lives they cease to be private citizens; they become game players who must be guided by a somewhat different set of ethical standards. . . .

The illusion that business can afford to be guided by ethics as conceived in private life is often fostered by speeches and articles containing such phrases as, 'It pays to be ethical,' or, 'Sound ethics is good for business.'

Actually this is not an ethical position at all; it is a self-serving calculation in disguise. The speaker is really saying that in the long run a company can make more money if it does not antagonize competitors, suppliers, employees, and customers by squeezing them too hard. He is saying that oversharp policies reduce ultimate gains. This is true, but it has nothing to do with ethics.

To be a winner, a man must play to win. This does not mean that he must be ruthless, cruel, harsh, or treacherous. On the contrary, the better his reputation for integrity, honesty, and decency, the better his chances of victory will be in the long run. But from time to time every businessman, like every poker player, is offered a choice between certain loss or bluffing within the legal rules of the game. If he is not resigned to losing, if he wants to rise in his company and industry, then in such a crisis he will bluff – and bluff hard.

Whatever the form of the bluff, it is an integral part of the game, and the executive who does not master its techniques is not likely to accumulate much money or power.

(Adapted extracts from: Carr, A. Z. (1968) 'Is business bluffing ethical?' *Harvard Business Review*, 46 (1), pp. 143–53.)

A3 What should you write down?

Why bother making notes?

Writing good essays involves a continuous process of thinking, reading and writing, and making notes is an important part in this cycle. The mental and physical process of making notes helps you to understand, think and reflect on what you have read. Making notes also helps you to formulate thoughts and ideas, to make connections in your mind with other pieces of knowledge, and to remember information.

Importantly, the writing process of making notes also helps you to start using your own words, which is essential for when you come to writing your essay. Making notes helps you to develop thinking that is less dependent on the text and helps you to control how you use your sources rather than letting your sources control your essay.

For all these reasons, students who make notes on their reading usually get better marks than those who go straight from reading a text to essay writing. However, for your notes to be really effective, they need to be clear, meaningful and of real use to you in the essay writing stage. This section gives you some steps, examples and practice to help you write effective notes.

Three key steps for making notes

Step 1   Write down the reference details
You should already have written down details such as the author, title and date of each source (called the reference or bibliographic details) when you found them. For books this should include the publishing company and where it was published. These days we are all used to getting bits of information from the media and websites without always knowing or needing to know where the information came from. However, for academic writing and work, knowing exactly who wrote something and where the text can be found is vital, as people actually own the knowledge or ideas they have written about.

Write down the bibliographic information accurately and be particularly careful not to change capital letters or punctuation in the titles of books or articles. At this stage you don't need to worry about the order of the information, just make sure you record it fully and accurately.

You should also write down where and how you found your sources. This will save you time if you need to go back to check a source and will help you find new sources in the future. You can simply write down these details in a notebook or save the information electronically.

Below is an example of the student's research record (also called a research log) for the article by Albert Carr. The student found the article by using an e-database on 20 November 2008.

> Reference details:
> Albert Z. Carr. 1968. 'Is business bluffing ethical?' Harvard Business Review. Vol. 46 Issue 1, pages 143–153.
>
> Research details:
> HBR is a peer-reviewed acad. journal. Got ref. from list at back of Crane and Matten 2007.
> Found it on 20/11/08 in Infolinx → Business Source Complete → Business Resources → Titles → HBR.

Step 2 Make notes on your reading

People make notes in different ways and you may like to use diagrams, flow charts, bullet points or index cards. You may want to make notes on only parts of the text, on one particular aspect of the text or on the whole text, depending on why you are reading it.

Whatever method you use to take notes, you should always:

- Write down the reference details, page numbers (particularly for quotations) and the date on which you make your notes.
- Read carefully and make accurate notes – don't accidentally change the meaning of the text.
- Make clear in your notes which ideas are major points, which are only examples of these major points and which are more minor points of information.
- Make sure your notes are not too brief *or* too detailed.
  If your notes are too brief, the meaning will be unclear and you won't understand them in a month's or year's time. If your notes are too detailed then it probably means you are copying too much – note taking does not mean copying whole sections from the text.
- Try to use some of your own words and abbreviations.
  You may be worried about changing the meaning of the text accidentally, of 'moving away' from the text, or you may feel that you can't put things into your own words as well as the original. However, if you are reading thoughtfully and with understanding rather than just copying, you will naturally start using some of your own words. It is important that you start doing this, and your confidence will increase with practice.

- Have a system which allows you to clearly see in your notes where you have used:

  exact words from the text (quotations);

  most of the same words from the text (close paraphrase);

  your *own* words to describe ideas in the text (paraphrase);

  your own ideas or comments.

  You must record these differences carefully so that when you use your notes to write your essay, you do not accidentally claim words or ideas from your sources as your own. Clearly recording your *own* thoughts will also help you to make full use of them and so get credit for them in your work.

Step 3   Write a short reflection from your notes

When you have finished making your notes, use them (and your critical analysis) to write a short reflection. Your reflection can be informal and take any form that you find helpful. However, it is a good idea to write in your own words and in full sentences and to use quotation marks for exact phrases from the original text. Your reflection should include a short summary of what you have learnt. If the text has a diagram or table, try to summarise what it shows in one sentence. Your reflection should also include your thoughts from your questioning, evaluation and location of the text.

Writing a short reflection from your notes will consolidate your reading, thinking, questioning and note taking and will maximise the effectiveness of the whole process. It will help you to restate information and ideas from your sources in your own words and will enable you to further develop your own ideas. It will help you to relate what you have read to what you already know and will put you in a position where you can see how and where you want to use your sources in your essay.

● Looking at an example of some notes

Below are the student's notes from the sections of the Svensson and Wood article on pages 15–16.

	Svensson, G. and Wood, G. (2008) 'A Model of Business Ethics'. *Journal of Business Ethics*, 77, pp. 303–322 Notes written on 1/3/2009
p. 310 true? no model?	In 30 yrs of BE as a subject, no model of BE – S + W want to fill this gap in BE theory, for debate.
p. 310 does it? – don't think so.	'Socially responsible managers do the right thing because it is the right thing to do'. Soc. expects the correct action. (CP)
p. 319 (conclusion)	Mangs. should want to be ethical because it brings success and freedom. (S + W citing Thomas et al. 2004)

p. 319 main point	BE– '. . . dynamic and continuous process . . .' – 'interrelationship between businesses and society . . .' – each responsible for the other.
good point re. importance of BE	BE becoming impt. because people feel that buss. do <u>not</u> behave ethically ∴ the 'mutual obligations need to be restated' (from Hoffman and Moore 1982).

Comments on the notes

- The student's notes are brief but contain enough detail to be meaningful. If the first line of the notes had been *In 30 yrs no model – S + W want to fill this gap*, this would have been too brief and when reading these notes at a later stage the student would have been asking himself: '30 years of what?' 'A model of what?' 'What type of gap do they want to fill?'
- Notice how the student has a clear system for recording which parts of his notes are quotation, close paraphrase or paraphrase and which are his own thoughts. First, he has used the margin for page numbers and for his own comments and ideas. Secondly, he has put phrases and key words taken from the text in quotation marks and has been careful to write down quotes accurately, using three dots to indicate when a quotation is not a whole sentence. He has also noted the details of when Svensson and Wood have quoted other authors (Thomas et al. and then Hoffman and Moore). Finally, he has used the letters CP (close paraphrase) to remind himself when he has used *mostly* the same words as the text. This is important, as he will need to put these ideas much more into his own words if he wants to use them in his essay.
- You can see that in making notes the student has naturally started the process of using his own words and phrases.

● Looking at an example of a short reflection

Below is a short reflection on the Svensson and Wood article, which the student wrote after reading and critically analysing the text and then making and re-reading his notes. You will notice that by now he is using mostly his own words and style of expression.

> The authors propose and describe their own model of business ethics which centres around a 'dynamic and continuous process' between business and society. They argue persuasively that business and society influence each other, are dependent on each other and have a responsibility to each other. Importantly, they stress that the ethical standards of society are also those of business and that therefore business ethics is important.
> Their model assumes that individuals and society always expect businesses to

behave well and that we should be able to trust businesses. Svensson and Wood also assume that good managers exist who are socially responsible. I think that these assumptions may be true some of the time but are ove-simplistic.

However, their model is well-researched and comprehensive and is supported by a great deal of other research in the field and their idea of an 'interrelationship between business and society' accords with Esty, Collins and Shaw and Barry. I agree with them that the way businesses behave does affect society and vice versa and I will use Svensson and Wood as a key source to support my argument that business ethics are important.

Practice 3: Make notes and write a reflection

Before you can come up with your own system for making clear and meaningful notes, you need to be aware of how you normally *do* take notes. To do this, read and make notes on the extracts from the article by Carr on page 17 (or use a short text of your own choice if you prefer). Read your notes a week later and compare them with the original text. Check for the following:

- Is the meaning clear in your notes?
- Can you distinguish between major and minor points?
- Have you copied down the exact words from the text; have you used a mixture of your own and the author's words; or have you used your own words? Is it clear which is which?
- If anything is unclear, how could you improve the way you take notes so that you really would be able to use them accurately and effectively in an essay?

After you have reviewed and improved your notes, use both your notes and critical reading of the text to write a short reflection. You can compare your notes with the student notes on page 123 although, as stated, there is no one correct way of taking notes.

A4 Why and how should you quote?

● **Why use quotations?**

Quotations are *exact* phrases or sentences taken from your reading. Below is a section from the business ethics essay which includes a quotation (given in blue).

> Many companies list only the quality, naturalness and sustainability of their products as their underlying ethical message. One example of a company statement which also includes the human dimension is the following: 'we will operate our business with a strong commitment to the well being of our fellow humans and the preservation of the planet' (Body Shop International, Policy on donations, May 2006, p. 1).

Most of the time you should use your reading in your essay by reinterpreting it in your own words. Only use exact words or phrases from a text for something which you think is particularly interesting or well expressed. Quotations can be a powerful tool in writing a good essay but only if you use them sparingly and for the right reasons.

Reasons to quote
Use quotations to:

- give a definition;
- state a fact or idea that the author has expressed in a unique and powerful way;
- establish or summarise an author's argument or position;
- provide an interesting and important start or end to your essay.

Reasons *not* to quote
Don't quote someone just because:

- you think that putting quotations in your essay will make it look academic and will impress your tutor;
- some of the articles you have read used lots of quotations so you think your essay should too;
- you have written half of your essay and haven't used any quotations yet so

you think you should put some in;
- you haven't given enough time to reading critically and taking notes, so it seems much easier to cut and paste some quotations into your essay rather than putting things into your own words.

How many quotations should you use?

A mistake students often make is to use too many quotations. The important thing is to think about *why* you are quoting, not how much. An essay may not have *any* quotations (or very few) but may still be a powerful and successful piece of work because the student has expressed her sources effectively using her own words. Indeed, using too many quotations (for more than a quarter of your essay, for example) is a type of plagiarism, even if you have put in all the correct in-essay references and quotation marks. This is because you can't really claim that your essay is your own work if it is made up mainly of quotations from other people. The number of quotations you decide to use will also depend on your subject area and your essay title; the business ethics essay, for example, has about 6 per cent of its word count as quotation.

● Looking at examples of using quotations effectively

Below are three extracts from the business ethics essay which contain quotations (given in blue, with in-essay reference features in red). Read the extracts and think about why the student decided to quote from his reading.

1   Shaw and Barry (2007) define business ethics as 'the study of what constitutes right and wrong (or good and bad) human conduct in a business context' (p. 25). Another definition describes business ethics as the 'principles and standards that guide behaviour in the world of business' (Ferrell and Fraedrich et al., 2002, p. 6).

2   Others such as Wolf share this view, and Prindl and Prodham (1994) suggest that 'Finance as practised in the professions and in industry is seen as a value-neutral positive discipline promoting efficiency without regard to the social consequences which follow from its products' (p. 3).

3   Secondly, an even stronger argument for the view that good ethics in business do in fact exist, is that given by Collins (1994) and other prominent experts on the subject. This is that 'good ethics is synonymous with good management' (p. 2).
   (*et al.* = and the other authors.)

Comments on the quotations

The student decided to quote in extract 1 to give examples of different academic definitions of business ethics. In extract 2 he decided to quote to demonstrate his point that some academics and business people feel that business should not concern itself with ethics. The student also felt that this particular sentence from Prindl and Prodham was an important and well-expressed statement.

In extract 3 the student used the quotation to support the main point of his essay, that business ethics is central to business. He also felt that the statement was a very strong and clear summary by Collins of this idea.

Note that in all three extracts, the student has introduced the quotation clearly so that the reader understands why it has been used. In other parts of his essay, the student quoted two individual words, *bluffing* and *dysfunctional*, because he felt that these were key words used by the authors in a unique way.

● Four key steps for using quotations properly

Step 1
Being able to use quotations effectively starts from when you select and read with questions in mind, critically evaluate, take meaningful notes and reflect on how you will use your reading in your essay. If you follow this process, you should be able to make good choices in what to quote.

Step 2
Before you put a quotation into your essay, ask yourself *why* you are putting it in. Is it special enough? Is it really relevant to your point? Would it not be better to put it into your own words?

Step 3
When you have written the first draft of your essay, separate out each quotation with its surrounding sentences. Read the quotation and its surrounding sentences slowly and carefully. Have you introduced the quotation clearly? Does it clearly support your point?

Step 4
Once you are sure that your quotation is worth putting in, check that you have quoted accurately, that you have used quotation marks *and* an in-essay reference and that you have used the correct grammar and punctuation before, during and after the quotation.

● Four common mistakes students make with the content of quotations

The four most common and serious mistakes students make are:

- using a quotation that is not special enough and where they should therefore have used their own words. This includes common facts or knowledge, which don't usually need to be quoted;
- using a quotation that does not directly support the student's point;

- not introducing or showing clearly why a quotation has been used;
- using a reporting verb (e.g. *states, shows, suggests, points out, claims*) which is not correct for the context and function of the quotation (we will look at this type of mistake in more detail in Section B2).

Practice 4: Would you use these quotations?

Below are some quotations from student essays on bioscience topics. Read them and identify which of the above mistakes the students have made.

1   Kzanty (2004) states that 'Organs such as the heart, liver, small bowel, pancreas and lungs are used for transplants' (p. 11).

2   Logan (1999) states that 'The second world war ended in 1945' (p. 111).

3   The main benefit or organ transplant is that it saves lives. As stated by Smith (2005), 'heart transplantation can save lives, but the procedure carries serious risks and complications and a high mortality rate' (p. 12).

4   Improvements in transplantation have made it possible for animal organs to be used. This is beneficial, as patients are not forced to wait for transplants. As stated by Kline (2005): 'advances in genetic techniques mean that there is less chance of animal organs being rejected by the human immune system' (p. 53).

5   Transplantation carries the risk of being attacked by the immune system and the patient is therefore at risk of organ failure. As stated by Smith (2005): 'Everyone reported common side effects which included diarrhoea, edemas, fatigue and ulcers' (p. 5).

● **Three common mistakes students make with in-essay references for quotations**

The three most common and serious mistakes students make when referencing quotations are:

- Forgetting that you must use quotation marks **and** an in-essay reference.

Some students make the mistake of using quotation marks but do not give an in-essay reference, because they think that the quotation marks and a reference in the bibliography at the end of the essay are enough. Other students make the mistake of giving a quotation with an in-essay reference but no quotation marks, because they think that the in-essay reference is enough.

The rules of writing at university are that if you use another person's words, you must always indicate this with quotation marks *and* an in-essay reference, as well as a reference in the bibliography. If you give an in-essay reference without quotations marks, it is always assumed that you are expressing an idea from a source but *in your own words*. Therefore, quoting without using quotation marks is plagiarism (claiming someone else's words or ideas as your own) even if you have given an in-essay reference. The only time you do not use quotation marks is for long quotations of more than three sentences; for these quotations indentation is used to show that you are using someone else's words.

Look again at the essay extract below and notice how the student introduces the quotation, gives an in-essay reference (including the page number) *and* uses quotation marks.

> Another definition describes business ethics as the 'principles and standards that guide behaviour in the world of business' (Ferrell and Fraedrich et al., 2002, p. 6).

- Giving an in-essay reference for a primary source when you have only read the secondary source.

You must make clear in your essay which book or article you have actually read. In the correct example below, the student has used the phrase *cited in* to show that he did not read the Hoffman and Moore article itself but read their quotation in the article by Svensson and Wood. It would be poor scholarship and a misrepresentation of what you have read to give only the reference for Hoffman and Moore.

> Hoffman and Moore (1982) suggest that the public feels that businesses fail to behave in a socially acceptable manner and that '. . . the mutual obligations of business to the community and the community to business need to be restated' (Hoffman and Moore, 1982, cited in Svensson and Wood, 2008).

- Putting brackets in the wrong place.

Look again at the extract from the business ethics essay below. Notice that for the first quotation the student uses Shaw and Barry as part of his introductory sentence, so he only puts brackets around the year of publication and for the page number. For the second quotation, however, the student does not use the authors Ferrell and Fraedrich et al. as part of his sentence, so both the names and year of publication are in brackets at the end of the quotation.

Shaw and Barry (2007) define business ethics as 'the study of what constitutes right and wrong (or good and bad) human conduct in a business context' (p. 25). Another definition describes business ethics as the 'principles and standards that guide behaviour in the world of business' (Ferrell and Fraedrich et al., 2002, p. 6).

Practice 5: Are these quotations referenced properly?

Below are four incorrect versions of the first part of the essay extract above. Look at these altered versions and identify what the mistakes are in the way these quotations have been referenced.

1   Business ethics is the study of what constitutes right and wrong (or good and bad) human conduct in a business context.

2   Shaw and Barry (2007) define business ethics as the study of what constitutes right and wrong (or good and bad) human conduct in a business context (p. 25).

3   Business ethics is 'the study of what constitutes right and wrong (or good and bad) human conduct in a business context'.

4   (Shaw and Barry, 2007) define business ethics as 'the study of what constitutes right and wrong (or good and bad) human conduct in a business context'.

● Four common mistakes students make with grammar and punctuation in quotations

The most common mistakes students make with the grammar and punctuation of quotations are:

●   Changing some of the words in the quotation.

You cannot change *any* words in a quotation. If you want to miss out part of the quotation use three dots (called 'ellipsis') to indicate that you have left out some words. If you need to add a word of your own to make the quotation fit with its surrounding sentence or to clarify meaning, use a square bracket to show that you have added something which was not in the original text, for example: Emille (2002) states that 'They [the public] only hear what they want to hear' (p. 10).

- Putting in an extra 'he/she/it/they' or topic word before a quotation.

  If you use the author's name as part of your sentence you do not need to also use 'he/she/it/they/their' in the introductory sentence. Equally, if you use the topic word (e.g. 'business ethics') in your introductory sentence, you should not repeat it in the quotation.

- Changing the first letter of a quotation from lower case (e.g. *we*) to upper case (e.g. *We*).

  If your quotation is not the start of a sentence in the original, do not change the first letter to a capital letter in your quotation – keep everything exactly as it is in the original text.

- Putting punctuation marks in the wrong place at the end of a quotation.

  Don't worry too much about making small mistakes with the punctuation of quotations but do try to develop correct use over time. Keep question marks and other punctuation from the original text *inside* the quotation marks. The exception to this is the full-stop; for the author/year in-essay reference style you should put the full-stop at the very end, after the page number brackets.

Practice 6: Is the grammar and punctuation of these quotations correct?

Below is one of the extracts from the business ethics essay followed by four incorrect versions. Identify the mistakes in each incorrect version. The answer section includes a correct version of this extract using a numeric referencing system.

Correct extract
Secondly, an even stronger argument for the view that good ethics in business do in fact exist, is that given by Collins (1994) and by other prominent experts on the subject. This is that 'good ethics is synonymous with good management' (p. 2).

Incorrect versions
1 Secondly, an even stronger argument for the view that good ethics in business do in fact exist, is that given by Collins (1994) and by other prominent experts on the subject. This is that 'good business ethics is synonymous with good management' (p. 2).

2 Secondly, an even stronger argument for the view that good ethics in

business do in fact exist, is that given by Collins (1994) and by other prominent experts on the subject. This is that 'good ethics is good management' (p. 2).

3 Secondly, an even stronger argument for the view that good ethics in business do in fact exist, is that given by Collins (1994) and by other prominent experts on the subject. This is that good ethics 'good ethics is synonymous with good management' (p. 2).

4 Secondly, an even stronger argument for the view that good ethics in business do in fact exist, is that given by Collins (1994) and by other prominent experts on the subject. This is that 'good ethics is synonymous with good management.' (p. 2)

A5 Why and how should you use your own words?

Paraphrasing is when you express ideas and information from your sources in your own way, using your own words. The ability to paraphrase well is central to university study and writing, and is also an ability which employers look for in graduates. This section gives you essential points on paraphrasing, takes you through some examples of good and poor paraphrasing and gives you a short practice exercise to help you acquire this complex skill.

● Why paraphrase?

Restating what you have read, in your own way, is one of the most fundamental aspects of all academic writing because it allows you to:

- go through a mental process which helps you to understand and think about what you read in a more independent way;
- express the information and ideas from sources in your own style of thinking and writing so that you can integrate them smoothly into your own argument and essay;
- restate information and ideas from your sources in a way that best supports your own argument;
- show your tutor that you have understood what you have read and that you have used your reading to develop your knowledge and ideas;
- express information and ideas from complicated texts more clearly and simply;
- restate information and ideas from your sources which are not special enough to quote.

● Looking at examples of good paraphrasing

Below are two extracts from one of the books the student read for his business ethics essay. Each extract is followed by the section in this essay where he introduces his own point and then paraphrases the source (in blue). Read and compare the source extracts with the essay extracts.

Source extract 1

There has also been an outpouring of books, magazine, journal and newspaper articles on the subject, as well as web pages, blogs, and other electronic publications – amazon.com currently stocks more than 2,000 books related to business ethics and corporate responsibility, whilst a google search on 'business ethics' returns more than 4 million hits at the time of writing. . . . One annual UK survey, for instance, estimates the country's 'ethical market' (i.e. consumer spending on ethical products and services) to be worth something like €40bn annually.

(Extract from: Crane, A. and Matten, D. (2007) *Business Ethics*, p. 14.)

Essay extract 1

The subject of business ethics has become increasingly important over the past few decades and now appears to be a prevalent factor in consumer choice. . . . The UK ethical market is valued at over 40 billion euros per year and there are currently over 2,000 books and 4 million web entries related to business ethics (Crane and Matten, 2007).

Source extract 2

. . . there is indeed considerable overlap between ethics and the law. In fact, the law is essentially and institutionalisation or codification of ethics into specific social rules, regulations, and proscriptions. Nevertheless, the two are not equivalent. . . . The law might be said to be a definition of the minimum acceptable standards of behaviour. However, many morally contestable issues, whether in business or elsewhere, are not explicitly covered by the law. . . . In one sense then, business ethics can be said to begin where the law ends. Business ethics is primarily concerned with those issues not covered by the law, or where there is no definite consensus on whether something is right or wrong.

(Extract from: Crane, A. and Matten, D. (2007) *Business Ethics*, pp. 5 and 7.)

Essay extract 2

When describing what business ethics is, it is essential to clarify that it is not synonymous with the law or with morals in general. Although the law overlaps with ethics, it usually only regulates the lowest level of acceptable behaviour (Crane and Matten, 2007). In fact, business ethics is mainly concerned with issues and areas of business conduct which are *not* specifically covered by the law and which are therefore vulnerable to exploitation and to what is viewed as immoral behaviour, even though it may be legal (ibid.).

(*ibid.* means that this source is exactly the same as the one previously referred to.)

Comments on the paraphrases

Notice how the student has not just replaced individual words in his paraphrases. His paraphrases are a complete rewriting of the source, based on his independent understanding, and written from his notes in his own style so that they make sense to him. His paraphrases are less complex than the original and he has changed the order of the information.

In essay extract 2, the student has emphasised the fact that ethics is not the same thing as the law. He has emphasised this difference because in this part of his essay he is defining and describing what business ethics is and so wants to point out the differences between ethics, the law and morals.

Notice that both paraphrases are shorter than the original. A paraphrase may be as long and as detailed as the original text but may also be shorter because you have condensed the points and used simpler language. The paraphrase in essay extract 1 is shorter than the original extract because the student has used this paraphrase in his essay introduction as only a brief example of the importance of business ethics. Paraphrase 2 is also shorter than the original extract because although the student has included all the points from the original text, he has used simpler language and condensed the ideas in his own way.

● Five key points to remember when you are paraphrasing

1 Check that your paraphrase clearly supports the point *you* are making.
Don't let your paraphrases take control of your essay. Decide what point you want to make and then check that your paraphrase is relevant and that it supports your point. You would normally only paraphrase short sections from a source as support for your own thoughts and ideas. Check that you have expressed the information and used reporting verbs (e.g. *show*, *suggest*, *claim*) in such a way as to give the emphasis which best supports your argument.

2 Write your paraphrase from your notes and reflection, not straight from the original text.
If you have approached your reading in a similar way to that suggested in Sections A1, A2 and A3, you will already be more than halfway to writing good paraphrases. Your paraphrase should be your own understanding and rewriting of short sections of a source, not a translation straight from the text.

3 Use your own words and writing style.
When you paraphrase you must use your own words as far as possible – around 90% of the wording should be your own. The rules of academic writing do not allow you to change only a few words, and even changing about half of the words from the original text still counts as plagiarism. You must either change nothing and use the source as a quotation, or rewrite the source as a paraphrase, using over 90% of your own words. The word order and pattern of the sentences should also be your own as far as possible. Finding your own words will be much easier if you have gone through the process of taking good notes and writing a reflection on your reading.

●   Keeping words from the original text.

There will be some words or short phrases you can't change; in the example para-phrases these words are *business ethics, ethical market, law* and *behaviour.* You do not need to put quotation marks around such commonly used words. However, if you are keeping a word from the source which the author has used in a unique or special way, or if the word is a new term which the author has invented, you should use it as a one-word quotation and put quotation marks around it. Always check that you have not accidentally used the same words or sentence patterns as the original text unless absolutely necessary.

You should also try to rephrase statistics. For example, *one fifth* can also be expressed as *20%,* and *more than double* can be expressed as *over twice as many/much.* It may not always be possible or make sense to rephrase numbers and statistics but you should do this if you can.

In order to paraphrase, you will need to know an adequate number of words commonly used in academic writing and be able to use them in a precise way. We will look at this vocabulary in Part B.

4   Always use an in-essay reference.

Using in-essay references with your paraphrases is essential, not optional. You must *always* give in-essay references when paraphrasing because the ideas and information you have restated are not yours, even though you have used your own words.

One of the most common types of accidental plagiarism is when students para-phrase but do not give an in-essay reference, because they think that using their own words means that they do not need to reference. However, paraphrasing without giving an in-essay reference is plagiarism, because if something is not referenced, it is assumed to be both your own words *and* your own idea.

Giving in-essay references is also an important way of getting marks. Your in-essay references will show your tutor that you have done some reading and that you have understood it. In-essay references also show your tutor (and yourself) how the authors you have read have helped to develop your own ideas. Finally, using in-essay references shows that you know where your own essay is located in your subject area.

5   Use reference reminder phrases.

Giving an in-essay reference at the start of your paraphrase will often not be enough. In essay extracts 1 and 2 above, the student gives an in-essay reference at the end of the first sentence of each paraphrase. This is adequate for paraphrase 1 because it is only one sentence long. For paraphrase 2 however, the student also puts *ibid.* at the end of the second sentence to make clear that the idea in the second sentence also comes from Crane and Matten rather than himself.

Below is an example of another section from the business ethics essay, where the student paraphrases from Carr. The student has used the reference reminder phrase *he suggests that* to make clear that the ideas in the second sentence are still those of Carr.

Carr (1968) uses the analogy of a poker game to argue that a successful busi-nessman needs to play by the rules of business in which 'bluffing' is an accept-able form of behaviour and that these rules are distinct from personal or social values. He suggests that even if a manager claims that good ethical conduct is also good for business, s/he is not really making a choice to be ethical but is merely using ethical conduct as a profitable business strategy.

If you don't use reference reminder phrases, it may become unclear in your essay which of your sentences express your own ideas and which ones express the ideas of other authors. This lack of clarity could lead you to accidentally plagiarise because, as stated above, it is always assumed in academic writing that anything which is not referenced is your own comment or idea.

How much paraphrasing should you do in an essay?

The amount you paraphrase in an essay will depend on how many sources you use and this will depend on your essay title and subject matter. If you are conducting your own experiment or research, you may not be using many sources and therefore may not be paraphrasing. However, most types of undergraduate essay and writing will consist of many short paraphrases from different sources. If you look at some acade-mic journal articles in your subject you will see that some of them consist of a total of up to 50% paraphrase (from lots of different sources and therefore with lots of different in-essay references). The business ethics essay has about 60% of its word count as paraphrase. Note that this essay is still original to the student because of which sources he has decided to use and how he has used them.

Four common mistakes students make when paraphrasing

- Not showing clearly where a paraphrase begins and ends.
  Student essays often do not show clearly enough which sentences are their own words and ideas and which sentences are paraphrases of sources. For example, if you only give one in-essay reference in brackets at the end of a long paragraph, it probably won't be clear which sentences in that paragraph are paraphrase and which sentences are your own ideas. As discussed in the key points above, you must use both in-essay references and reference reminder phrases.

- Not making enough changes from the original source.
  Students sometimes use just a few of their own words to 'sew together' unchanged sentences or phrases from a source or from several different sources. Even if you give the relevant in-essay references, this type of 'sewing' is plagiarism because the words and style of most of the sentences are not your own.

- Changing individual words but keeping the same sentence pattern as the original.

    This might happen if you don't take notes and reflect on your reading but just try to 'translate' word by word from the text straight into your essay. Even if you change all the words, your paraphrase will still have the same style and pattern as the original text and this is still therefore a type of plagiarism.

- Accidently changing the meaning of the original text.

    This might happen if you have not read and understood the text carefully enough or thought critically about it, or have not made clear notes. Make sure you understand from the text what is fact and what is opinion, and pay particular attention to small but important words such as *no*, *not* or *not as* and comparatives such as *faster*. For example, saying that smoking cannabis is *not as* damaging as smoking cigarettes is very different from saying that smoking cannabis is not damaging.

● Looking at some examples of poor paraphrasing

Below is a short extract from a journal article which looks at whether mobile phones are a health risk.

The extract is followed by three unacceptable paraphrases which all try to use the article to support the view that mobile phones do not damage health. Read the extract and then the unacceptable paraphrases. Finally, read the comments and example of a good paraphrase of the article extract.

Source extract

So far there is no clear evidence from health studies of a relation between mobile phone use and mortality or morbidity. Indeed, tantalising findings in humans include a speeding up of reaction time during exposure, particularly during behavioural tasks calling for attention and electrical brain activity changes during cognitive processes. It is not clear, however, whether these findings have any positive implications for health.

(Adapted from: Maier, M., Blakemore, C. and Koivisto, M. (2000) 'The health hazards of mobile phones'. *British Medical Journal*, 320 (7245), pp. 1288–1289.)

Unacceptable paraphrases

1 Maier et al. (2000) show that there is no clear evidence from health studies of a relation between mobile phone use and mortality or morbidity. They state that in fact, tantalising findings in humans include a speeding up of reaction time during exposure, particularly during behavioural tasks calling for attention and changes in brain electricity during cognitive processes. It is not clear, however, whether these findings have any positive implications for health.

2   Some studies point to interesting results which suggest that while using a phone, the user has quicker reaction times to some behavioural tasks (Maier et al., 2000). In fact, there are interesting findings in humans that show a speeding up of reaction time during exposure, particularly during behavioural tasks calling for attention and changes in brain electricity during cognitive processes. It is unclear whether these findings have any positive implications for health.

3   Maier et al. (2000) show that up to now there is not any strong proof from studies on disease, of a link between the use of mobile phones and death or disease. In fact, interesting results in humans include a faster time of reaction during use, especially while doing practical tasks that need concentration and brain electricity change during the thought process. It is unclear whether these results imply any health benefits (ibid.)

(*Maier et al.* means 'Maier and other authors'.)

Comments on the unacceptable paraphrases

Paraphrase 1
The student has correctly used an in-essay reference and the reference reminder phrase *They state that*. However, the only changes she has made from the source are to put in these references, take off the first two words and reword the phrase 'electrical brain activity changes'. Everything else is copied word for word from the source without any use of quotation marks. This is plagiarism.

Paraphrase 2
The student has used an in-essay reference and she has also made some significant changes in wording. However, there are two problems with this paraphrase. The first is that there are still several long phrases which are unchanged from the original source (underlined below). This could be seen as plagiarism. Secondly, there is no reference reminder phrase and so the reader is not sure whether the information in the second sentence comes from Maier et al. or from the student. By the time the reader gets to the third sentence, it could easily be assumed that the point expressed in this sentence is that of the student and this could therefore be seen as plagiarism. Indeed, this paraphrase counts as plagiarised on two counts: lack of referencing, and copied phrases from the original source.

> Some studies point to interesting results which suggest that while using a phone, the user has quicker reaction times to some behavioural tasks (Maier et al., 2000). In fact, there are interesting <u>findings in humans</u> that show <u>a speeding up of reaction time during exposure, particularly during behavioural tasks calling for attention</u> and changes in brain electricity <u>during cognitive processes</u>. It is unclear <u>whether these findings have implications for health.</u>

Paraphrase 3
The student has used nearly all her own words and has used two in-essay references.

However, she has merely translated the original, word by word, as she goes along. The student has been too dependent on her source and instead of making and using notes, has gone straight from reading the article to writing her paraphrase. The result is a paraphrase that has exactly the same 'pattern' as the original. This does not show a clear understanding of the original or control of her source and is a type of plagiarism.

An example of a good paraphrase of the extract

Studies point to interesting results which suggest that mobile phone users experience quicker reaction times to tasks which require both changes in electrical brain activity and concentration (Maier et al., 2000). Although it has not been shown that these effects represent actual benefits to health, there has equally been no data from any disease studies to suggest that mobile phones actually damage health in any way (ibid.).

Practice 7: What do you think of these paraphrases?

Below is a short extract from a different article on the issue of mobile phones and health risks. Underneath the extract are four unacceptable paraphrases. Read the extract and paraphrases and identify what is wrong with each paraphrase. (The example of a good paraphrase in the answer section is given using both the author/year and the numeric referencing system.)

Source extract

Mobile phones provide an interesting example of a source risk to health which may be largely non-existent but which cannot be totally dismissed. Such risks, when possibly serious and with long-term consequences, are typically dealt with by appeal to the so-called precautionary principle but, of course, precaution comes at a price.

(Cox, D. R. (2003) 'Communication of risk: health hazards from mobile phones'. *Journal of the Royal Statistical Society: Series A (Statistics in Society)*, 166 (2), pp. 214–246.)

Unacceptable paraphrases

1   Advising caution in the use of mobile phones is an example of a typical approach to the fear of a possible health risk which may be of a serious nature. Such an approach may have negative consequences, but is taken because although there may in fact be no health risk, this has not yet been proven.

2   Cox (2003) suggests that advising caution in the use of mobile phones is an example of a typical approach to the fear of a possible

health risk which may be of a serious nature. Such an approach may have negative consequences, but is taken because although there may in fact be no health risk, this has not yet been proven.

3 Advising caution in the use of mobile phones is an example of a typical approach to the fear of a possible health risk which may be of a serious nature. Such an approach may have negative consequences, but is taken because although there may in fact be no health risk, this has not yet been proven (Cox, 2003).

4 Mobile phones provide an interesting example of a source risk to health which may be largely non-existent but which cannot be totally dismissed (Cox, 2003). So far there is no clear evidence from health studies of a relation between mobile phone use and mortality or morbidity.

A6 Why and how should you summarise?

A summary is when you express the main points from a source in your own way, using your own words. Both paraphrasing and summarising require you to use your own words and in-essay references. The difference between paraphrasing and summarising is that a paraphrase expresses *all* the information contained in a short, specific part of a text, whereas a summary gives only the *main* points from a much larger section or from a whole text. Summarising is a complex skill and one that you will need both at university and in your future career. This section gives you key points and steps for summarising, looks at common problems and gives examples of good and poor summarising.

● Why summarise?

Summarising is a key element in writing essays and other types of assignment, and is important for the same reasons as those given for paraphrasing at the beginning of A5 on page 31.

A summary can be an even more powerful writing tool than a paraphrase, however, because it allows you to show that you have understood the key point of a text and that you can express this clearly in your own way. Summarising therefore allows you great control over how you use your sources.

There are two main reasons for giving a summary in your essay:

- ● to give evidence and support for your own argument;
- ● to give an overview of different sources and authors who support a particular position.

An overview of sources (sometimes called a 'literature review') is common near the beginning of an essay although you can give a brief overview of the literature at any stage in your essay when you are setting the scene for a point in your argument. Giving a summary of the position of key authors shows that you understand where they are located in the subject, i.e. which authors hold similar positions to those of yourself and of each other and which authors hold different viewpoints.

How long should a summary be?

The length and level of detail of your summary will depend on what you want it to do in your essay. A summary which includes all the main points of a text may be up to a third as long as the original text. Often however, you will want to give a very brief summary of only a few sentences or even just one phrase to express the key point of a text.

● Looking at some examples of good summaries

Below are two separate extracts that you will recognise from the business ethics essay. Read each extract and think about why and how the student has briefly summarised his sources in the essay (the summaries are in blue). Then read the comments on each extract.

Essay extract 1

Opponents of the concept of ethics in business include those who claim that making a profit is the only responsibility a business has to society (Friedman, 1970, cited in Fisher and Lovell, 2003). Others such as Wolf (2008) share this view and Prindl and Prodham (1994) suggest that 'Finance as practised in the professions and in industry is seen as a value-neutral positive discipline promoting efficiency without regard to the social consequences which follow from its products' (p. 3). Carr (1968) uses the analogy of a poker game to argue that a successful businessman needs to play by the rules of business, in which 'bluffing' is an acceptable form of behaviour, and that these rules are distinct from personal or social values.

Essay extract 2

Secondly, an even stronger argument for the view that good ethics in business do in fact exist, is that given by Collins (1994) and other prominent experts on the subject. This is that 'good ethics is synonymous with good management' (p. 2). Collins states that if managers only concern themselves with profit, they will in fact become 'dysfunctional'. This is because any business is made up of people: employees, customers and other stakeholders. He states that if businesses do not operate with a degree of trust, co-operation and consideration, they will be putting constraints on profitability. This idea of the interdependence of any business organisation is also supported by Shaw and Barry (2007), Green (1994), Fritzsche (2005) and Svensson and Wood (2008).

Comments on the extracts

In essay extract 1, the student summarises the view of Friedman in one sentence and then summarises the position of Wolf in only three words by stating that Wolf shares the same view. The student then uses a key quotation as a type of summary to state the position of Prindl and Prodham. The extract ends with a one-sentence summary of Carr's position. The essay extract gives an effective overview of key authors who oppose the concept of business ethics.

In essay extract 2, the student first establishes his own point by using a key quotation, which also acts as a summary of Collins' position. He then explains Collins' view in a bit more detail by giving a two-sentence summary. In the final sentence of the extract the student summarises the main point of six other authors in a phrase of only nine words: 'This idea of the interdependence of any business organisation . . .'. By doing this, the student shows that he understands that all of these texts have interdependence as their key point and that therefore these authors all hold a similar position on the issue.

Five key points to remember when you are summarising

- Express only the main point or points in the text.
- Give an objective and balanced summary of the key points and do not include your own opinion or comments.
- As with paraphrasing, your summary should be your own expression, style and words as far as possible. It is not acceptable to change only a few words of the original text or to sew together key sentences copied from the text (unless you use them as quotations).
- As with paraphrasing, you must always give in-essay references with your summary because the ideas and information you have restated are not yours, even though the way you have expressed them is. Summarising without giving an in-essay reference is a form of plagiarism.
- If your summary is more than one sentence long, check whether you need to use reference reminder phrases to make clear that the later sentences are still points from your source.

● Five key steps for writing good summaries

Step 1   Identify how the source text is organised

Writing a good summary starts with your reading. Make sure that you understand how the text is structured. Read the title, sub-headings, introduction and conclusion of the text to help you identify the key points. Identify which parts of the text are main points and which are examples of these points or more minor points.

Step 2   Understand, make clear notes and critically reflect on your reading

If you have approached your reading in a similar way to the steps given in Sections A1, A2 and A3, you will already be more than halfway to writing a good summary. If you have written a critical reflection on what you have read, you will probably have written a short summary as part of it.

Step 3   Summarise what the text is about in one or two sentences
A really useful exercise is to start by using your notes to write a very short summary consisting of only one or two sentences. Doing this helps you to clarify in your mind what the main point of the text is. You can then write a longer, more detailed summary that includes all the main points if you need to.

Step 4   Think about why and how you want to use the summary
Before you put your summary into your essay, ask yourself how it fits into your essay plan and argument. Make sure you use your summary to clearly support your own point.

Step 5   Check that you have used your own words and style, in-essay references and reference reminder phrases
As with paraphrasing, check that you have written your summary using your own words as far as possible and that you have used adequate in-essay referencing.

Six common mistakes students make when summarising

- accidently changing the meaning of the original text;
- giving too much detail and putting in minor points, examples or definitions from the text, rather than just the main points;
- adding their own opinion or comments;
- not making enough changes in words and style from the original source;
- not making clear where the summary begins and ends (i.e. not using clear in-essay references and reference reminder phrases);
- giving the primary source as the in-essay reference when they have only read a secondary source.

Practice 8: What is wrong with these summaries?

It is not possible in this book to give you a whole article or book to summarise. So, below is a short text written by J. Robinson in which she describes an article by Côté and Morgan.

Read the short text and make your own notes. Use your notes to write first a one-sentence summary of the text then a longer summary consisting of three or four sentences. (You may also like to use your notes to write a reflection – an example reflection is given in the answer section.)

After you have written your own summary, read the five unacceptable summaries and identify which common mistakes the students have made. Finally, read the comments on each summary.

A study on links between emotion regulation, job satisfaction and intentions to quit

Emotion regulation is the conscious and unconscious efforts people make to increase, maintain or decrease their emotions and is manifested by changes in facial expression and by changes in vocal and body signals. People often regulate their emotions at work. An example of emotion suppression is when a worker tries to hide anger they might be feeling towards a colleague or manager. Emotion amplification on the other hand, is when one pretends to be happier than one actually is. For example, an insurance or telephone salesperson may amplify their display of positive emotion to customers in order to increase their level of sales and quality of service.

Côté and Morgan (2002) conducted a study which looked at the relationship between emotion regulation, job satisfaction and intention to quit one's job. They collected two sets of data from 111 workers. The participants gave informed consent and were asked to complete two questionnaires on how they felt they had regulated their emotions at work and their feelings about their job. There was a time interval of four weeks between the two questionnaires to allow enough time for changes in emotion regulation and also to have a short enough period within which to retain the participants.

Côté and Morgan showed from their data that the amplification of pleasant emotions happened more frequently than the suppression of unpleasant emotions. Importantly, they also found a strong correlation between emotion regulation and job satisfaction and intention to quit. They demonstrated that, as they predicted, the suppression of unpleasant emotions leads to a decrease in job satisfaction and therefore an increase in intention to quit. Their findings also suggest that an increase in the amplification of pleasant emotions will increase job satisfaction, because it increases positive social interaction and more positive responses from colleagues and customers.

Although their experiment showed that emotion regulation affects job satisfaction, there was no strong evidence to suggest an opposite correlation, i.e. that job satisfaction and intention to quit influence emotional regulation.

Reference List
Côté, S. and Morgan, L. M. (2002) 'A longitudinal analysis of the association between emotion regulation, job satisfaction, and intentions to quit'. *Journal of Organizational Behaviour*, 23, pp. 947–962.

Text written by J. Robinson, 2008.

Unacceptable summaries

1   Emotion regulation is the conscious and unconscious efforts people make to increase, maintain or decrease their emotions. Côté and Morgan (2002) have conducted a study which looked at the relationship between emotion regulation, job satisfaction and intention to quit one's job. Côté and Morgan showed from their data that the amplification of pleasant emotions happened more frequently than the suppression of unpleasant emotions. Importantly, they also found a strong correlation between emotion regulation and job satisfaction and intention to quit.

2   A study has shown a strong link between emotion regulation and job satisfaction and intention to quit (Côté and Morgan, 2002, cited in Robinson, 2008). An example of emotion regulation is when someone attempts to hide the anger they feel towards their boss or when they pretend to be happier than they really are during a work meeting or when dealing with customers. Côté and Morgan tested 111 workers by asking them to complete two questionnaires at an interval of four weeks. They found that workers exaggerate positive emotions more than they hide negative feelings. The findings also showed that suppressing negative emotions leads to a decrease in job satisfaction and that amplifying positive emotions leads to more positive interaction at work and therefore more job satisfaction.

3   Robinson (2008) describes a study conducted by Côté and Morgan, in which they obtained data on emotion regulation from 111 workers. The findings suggest that workers exaggerate positive emotions more than they hide negative feelings and that there is strong evidence that how you feel about your job influences how you regulate your emotions at work.

4   A study has shown a strong link between emotion regulation and job satisfaction and intention to quit (Côté and Morgan, 2002, cited in Robinson, 2008) and that workers exaggerate positive emotions more than they hide negative feelings. This might be because workers are worried that if they show their negative feelings, they might not get promoted, or worse, that they may lose their job. The findings also showed that suppressing negative emotions leads to a decrease in job satisfaction and that amplifying positive emotions leads to more positive interaction at work and therefore more job satisfaction.

Comments on the unacceptable summaries

1   This summary consists of four key sentences copied word for word from the original text. This is therefore plagiarism. In addition to this, the student has only given an in-essay reference for Côté and Morgan, which implies that they have read the primary Côté and Morgan article, when in fact they have only read the Robinson text. This is a misrepresentation of what the student has read and of Côté and Morgan.

2   The first and the last two sentences of this summary are good, with a correct in-essay reference. However, in the middle of the summary the student has included different examples of what emotion regulation is and also details of the method of the study, neither of which should be in a summary.

3   This summary starts with a correct in-essay reference but it does not state the key point of the text. In addition to this, the last point in the summary is not correct – the study showed that emotion regulation can influence how you feel about your job but there was *no* evidence that job satisfaction affects emotion regulation.

4   This summary starts well, with a clear statement of the key point and a correct in-essay reference. However, the second sentence is the student's own idea of why workers might hide negative feelings, and this should not be part of the summary. Any comments or opinion by the student on the results of the Côté and Morgan study should come after the summary rather than mixed up within it.

An example of an acceptable one-sentence summary

A study has shown a strong link between regulating emotions at work and job satisfaction and intentions to quit (Côté and Morgan, 2002, cited in Robinson, 2008).

An example of an acceptable three-sentence summary

A study has shown a strong link between emotion regulation and job satisfaction and intention to quit (Côté and Morgan, 2002, cited in Robinson, 2008). The findings also demonstrated that workers exaggerate positive emotions more than they hide negative feel-ings. Côté and Morgan also found that suppressing negative emotions leads to less job satisfaction and that amplifying positive emotions leads to better social interaction at work and therefore more job satisfaction (ibid.).

A7 Putting it all together in your essay

This final section in Part A reviews the process of using sources and looks at how to integrate quotation, paraphrase and summary into an essay paragraph. It also gives you some final comments and advice on plagiarism and a practice exercise to help you become more aware of how you integrate sources into your own writing.

Throughout Part A we have used extracts from the business ethics essay as examples of how to use sources, and below is another colour-coded extract from the essay as a final example.

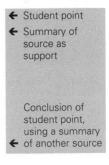

Clearly then, businesses are not isolated from society. Svensson and Wood (2008) show that the two are in fact mutually dependent and that both are responsible for the consequences and effects of the other as part of a constant two-way process. Their model importantly demonstrates that the ethical standards of society are also those of business. Carr's argument that business ethics are different and separate from the ethics of other social contexts does not seem to hold true.

← Student point
← Summary of source as support

Conclusion of student point, using a summary
← of another source

You should now be able to read the complete business ethics essay on pages 115–118 with a much clearer insight into why and how the sources have been used.

● Five key points to remember

- It is essential that you become really familiar with what you read so that you have a clear and independent understanding of it.
- Everyone approaches writing differently and there is not one correct way to write an essay. It is important that you care about your writing and that you feel it is your own individual piece of work. Even if you use lots of sources, it will be original because of *how* you have used them to answer the essay question.
- Get the best marks possible for your work by always giving in-essay references.
- An effective use of quotation, paraphrase and summary will enable you to control your sources and make them work for you in your essay.

- Confidence in quoting, paraphrasing and summarising will only come with practice.

Reviewing the whole process from reading your sources to writing your essay

To remind you of how the whole process works, Table 1 gives you each stage of using a short section of the Svensson and Wood article, with the relevant page numbers so that you can go back and review the stages in full. Note that at each stage the student increasingly interprets his source in his own way. Table 2 lists the relevant page numbers for using the Carr article.

Table 1   Stages in using the Svensson and Wood article

Stage 1   The article by Svensson and Wood. Pages 15–16.

. . . it is important to see business ethics as a highly dymanic and continuous process without an end. A process, however, that is predicated on the interrelationship between business and society where each one is interdependent and responsible together for the outcomes.

(Extract from: Svensson, G. and Wood, G. (2008) 'A Model of Business Ethics'. *Journal of Business Ethics*, 77, pp. 303–322.)

Stage 2   Student critical analysis. Page 16.

Svensson and Wood argue strongly and clearly that business and society influence each other and are dependent on each other and have a responsibility to each other to behave ethically. . . . I think that this article is solid enough to use as one of my main sources as evidence for what I think my conclusion will probably be.

Stage 3   Student notes. Pages 20–21.

BE – ' . . . dynamic and continuous process . . .' – 'interrelationship between business and society . . .' – each responsible for the other.

Stage 4   Student reflection. Pages 21–22.

The authors propose and describe their own model of business ethics which centres around a 'dynamic and continuous process' between business and society. They argue persuasively that business and society influence each other, are dependent on each other and have a responsibility to each other.

Stage 5   Paraphrase in the business ethics essay. Page 47.

Clearly then, businesses are not isolated from society. Svensson and Wood (2008) show that the two are in fact mutually dependent and that both are responsible for the consequences and effects of the other, as part of a constant two-way process. Their model importantly demonstrates that the ethical standards of society are also those of business.

Table 2	Stages in using the Carr article	
Stage 1	Article extract.	page 17
Stage 2	Critical analysis.	pages 122–123
Stage 3	Notes.	page 123
Stage 5	Paraphrase in essay.	page 35

Time management for each stage of the process

Figure 1 is a diagram which summarises each stage, from reading to essay, and which gives you an approximate minimum time you would need if you were searching online and using four journal articles. The precise time needed will be different for each individual and will depend on many different factors. However, one reason students get poor marks for their essays is that they have not given enough time to each part of the process, so you may find some rough time guidelines useful.

● A final word on plagiarism

Common causes of purposeful or accidental plagiarism are:

- not giving enough time to reading and understanding texts;
- not taking notes or writing a reflection;
- not understanding what counts as plagiarism in writing;
- lack of ability or confidence in restating something in your own words;
- not wanting to highlight the fact that you have used lots of sources;
- not giving clear in-essay referencing.

Part A of this book has taken you through key steps and practice exercises which address each of these issues. These sections have, hopefully, helped you to understand what plagiarism is and given you the knowledge and confidence to use your sources properly and effectively. Plagiarising will not do anything to help you learn and will not help you gain the skills you need for a good career. Even if your goal at university is only to get good marks, plagiarising is still a waste of time because plagiarised work is almost always of poor quality. It is easier and more enjoyable to do the work needed to produce a good essay yourself.

● Building your own house

You might find it helpful to think of the essay writing process in terms of designing and building a house (the house is your essay and the materials and fittings are your sources).

The first thing you would need to do is to be clear about the purpose of the house; why you were building it and what requirements you wanted it to meet. Even if you

Thinking; thoughts and ideas on the essay title.

Finding and selecting four relevant texts. Recording research details.

2 hours

Thinking

Reading, questioning, evaluating and locating the texts.

4 hours

Thinking

Re-reading and making clear and meaningful notes.

4 hours

Thinking

Writing a critical reflection on each text from your notes.

4 hours

Thinking

Deciding why and how you want to use the texts to support your argument.

1 hour

Thinking

Para-phrasing, summaris-ing and quoting the texts in your draft essay.

2 hours

Thinking

Checking that your sources precisely support your points and that you have used adequate rewriting and in-essay refer-encing.

1 hour

Figure 1 Time management for using your reading in your essay

had been given the basic design and requirements of the house (the essay title), you would still need to think about exactly how to meet the specifications of the design.

The materials for building the house (your sources) would need to be well researched, reliable and right for the job. The different materials and fittings you would use would mainly be ones that someone else had produced but the house would be original to you because of your design features, the materials and fittings you had decided to use, and how you had decided to use them. You would also keep receipts and manufacturer's details (a research log) in case of any problems and for use on future building projects.

When you had finished your house and were showing people round (anyone who reads your essay) they would be interested in who had designed and made various fittings such as the windows or kitchen units. You would, hopefully, be proud to answer their questions honestly. No-one would expect you to have made the kitchen units or windows yourself (and it would be obvious to anyone with any building experience that you had not done so). What would be important would be to show your intelligence and skill in finding and selecting materials, understanding how they worked and using them effectively in your own way to build your own house.

Practice 9: What do you think of the way these students have used this source in their essay?

Below are three paragraphs from three separate essays addressing the title: *In what ways might personality affect job satisfaction?*

All three students have used the text by J. Robinson on page 44. Read the three paragraphs and use the Robinson text to decide what the problem is in each case, then read the comments on each paragraph.

Finally, look at the example of a good paragraph, on page 53, in which the student has used their notes and reflection on the text as a basis for integrating the source information into their essay.

Unacceptable essay paragraphs

1   There does seem to be a link between personality and job satisfaction, although there are different views on how strong this link is. One interesting study on emotion regulation has demonstrated that there is a strong link between how we regulate our emotions at work and how satisfied we are with our jobs (Côté and Morgan, 2002, cited in Robinson, 2008). Their data showed that the amplification of pleasant emotions happened more frequently than the suppression of unpleasant emotions. Importantly, they also found a strong correlation between emotion regulation and job satisfaction and intention to quit. These findings would suggest that if you are good at regulating your emotions and particularly if you are able to

be (or at least pretend to be) positive, you are likely to have a higher level of job satisfaction than someone who cannot or does not want to amplify positive emotions. Although emotion regulation is not synonymous with personality, it seems likely that personality type is linked to emotion regulation and therefore to job satisfaction.

2   There does seem to be a link between personality and job satisfaction, although there are different views on how strong this link is. A study has shown that there is a strong link between how we regulate our emotions at work and how satisfied we are with our jobs. Workers exaggerate positive emotions more than they hide negative feelings. In addition, suppressing negative emotions leads to less job satisfaction and amplifying positive emotions leads to better social interaction at work and therefore more job satisfaction. If you are good at regulating your emotions and particularly if you are able to be (or at least pretend to be) positive, you are likely to have a higher level of job satisfaction than someone who cannot or does not want to amplify positive emotions. Although emotion regulation is not synonymous with personality, it seems likely that personality type is linked to emotion regulation and therefore to job satisfaction (Côté and Morgan, 2002, cited in Robinson, 2008).

3   Côté and Morgan claim that there is a strong link between emotion regulation and job satisfaction and intention to quit (Côté and Morgan, 2002, cited in Robinson, 2008). The findings showed that workers exaggerate positive emotions more than they hide negative feelings. Côté and Morgan also found that suppressing negative emotions leads to less job satisfaction and that amplifying positive emotions leads to better social interaction at work and therefore more job satisfaction.

Comments on the unacceptable essay paragraphs

1   This paragraph starts well, with the student introducing her own point that there is a link between personality and job satisfaction. She then starts to paraphrase the Robinson article and gives a correct in-essay reference. However, the third and fourth sentences are copied word for word from the Robinson text without any quotation marks; this is therefore plagiarism. The paragraph ends well with the student's own comments.

2   The student starts well by introducing her own point. She continues by summarising the Robinson text in her own words, which is good. However, she does not give any in-essay references or reference reminder phrases; this is plagiarism. After her summary she contin-

ues with her own comments on the implications of the study. Finally, she gives an in-essay reference in brackets at the end of the paragraph. This is inadequate referencing, as the reader would have no idea where the divisions were between the student's own points and her summary of the source.

3   This paragraph contains only the summary of the Robinson text. There are in-essay references but there is no introduction or conclusion by the student and we therefore have no idea of what point the student is trying to make. This is a case of the sources controlling the essay – the student has merely found sources she thinks might be relevant and put them in, without introducing them or thinking about what point she wants them to support in her essay.

Example of an acceptable essay paragraph using the Robinson text

There does seem to be a link between personality and job satisfaction, although there are different views on how strong this link is. One interesting study on emotion regulation has demonstrated that there is a strong link between how we regulate our emotions at work and how satisfied we are with our jobs (Côté and Morgan, 2002, cited in Robinson, 2008). The findings showed that workers exaggerate positive emotions more than they hide negative feelings. Côté and Morgan also found that suppressing negative emotions leads to less job satisfaction and that amplifying positive emotions leads to better social interaction at work and therefore more job satisfaction. These findings would suggest that if you are good at regulating your emotions and particularly that if you are able to be (or at least pretend to be) positive, you are likely to have a higher level of job satisfaction than someone who cannot or does not want to amplify positive emotions. The fact that if you suppress negative emotions, you will have less job satisfaction, suggests that if you are someone who can express negative feelings in a constructive way at work in order to find a solution to the problem, you will probably have more job satisfaction than someone who hides negative emotions without trying to resolve them. Although emotion regulation is not synonymous with personality, it seems likely that personality type is linked to emotion regulation and therefore to job satisfaction.

← Student point

← Summary of source used as evidence and support

← Student's ideas on the implications of the findings

← Conclusion of student's point

Part B Words and phrases to use

Introduction to Part B:
Why and how to build your vocabulary

In order to express information from sources in your own words and to integrate your reading into your essays, you need to know and use appropriate words and phrases precisely. Part B gives you examples of key words and phrases used in sentences, which will help you to develop your vocabulary and increase your ability and confidence in using your own words. This introduction explains the structure of Part B and also gives you important strategies and techniques for developing and using your vocabulary.

Each section in Part B will give you:

- 40–50 key words and phrases frequently used in academic writing. These are underlined and given in the context of a sentence. Words or phrases of similar meaning are grouped together;
- brief notes on words which are often used incorrectly by students;
- examples of student sentences which contain common vocabulary errors for you to correct using words given in that section;
- practice in using vocabulary in a precise way. Answers and explanatory notes for the practice exercises are given in Appendix 7.

Part B is a guide and resource for you to refer to when needed. Use the section titles and sub-headings to help you find what you want, and do some or all of the practice exercises that are most useful to you. Grammar points are explained only where necessary.

● Developing your formal vocabulary

Why use formal vocabulary?
The words and style used in academic texts and for university essays are described as 'formal'. One reason we use a formal written style is that it is internationally accepted and understood by scholars, students and other readers.

Another more important reason for using a fairly formal style of language is that it is clear and precise. Informal words and phrases such as *thing* or *make up* can have several different meanings, which often rely partly on the 'who, when and where' of the situation. However, when you are reading an academic article, you cannot speak to the author to ask them exactly what they mean in a particular sentence. Similarly, when your tutor is marking your essay, you will not be there to explain exactly what you meant; the finished essay you hand in is your last and only opportunity to be clear. We therefore use formal vocabulary in academic writing because it is commonly understood, is precise, and does not rely on physical location for its meaning.

If you are not familiar with formal academic writing style it can be difficult at first to judge just how formal to be. Some published books and articles use a style which is *too* complex and formal, and you should *not* try to be over-complicated or to use as many long words or sentences as possible. However, your writing *does* need to be clear and precise and so you do need to use a formal written style and vocabulary rather than the informal style we use when we speak. Section B6 will raise your awareness of the differences between formal and informal styles of writing.

A strategy for developing your vocabulary

Developing your formal vocabulary for academic work is not as hard as you might think, because there is a core of words (about 400–500) which are used repeatedly in academic texts across all subjects. Part A of this book uses about 200 core words and Part B gives you 260 more core words. You need to be able to understand what these words mean and to be able to *use* around 300–400 of them correctly and precisely in your own writing.

You probably already know what many of these words mean and you can probably use at least half of them. You therefore need to practise using the words you know in a precise way and also to gradually learn the meaning of new words. Your vocabulary will increase over the time of your course and beyond, and the simple fact is that the more you read and write, the more quickly you will learn and be able to use new words. Avoiding reading or not bothering to find out the meaning of useful new words will not develop your vocabulary.

You will be surprised how quickly you can learn and use new words if you do some or all of the following.

- Buy and *use* a good English–English dictionary (not pocket size). It is a good idea to buy one which gives words in example sentences. If used effectively, your dictionary will probably be the most useful book you ever buy. Read the dictionary guide which explains what the abbreviations used with word entries mean, as these give important information about how a word is used and whether it is formal or informal. An example of a dictionary entry and an explanation of abbreviations is given in Appendix 2.
- As you read a text, make a note of words and phrases that are frequently used and look them up in your dictionary to find out their precise meaning. If you are reading a text in electronic format, you may be able to use a 'find' function on your computer to highlight each time a particular word or phrase occurs so that you can see how it is commonly used in a sentence.

- Don't be tempted to read only easy textbooks, websites or magazine articles. Have the confidence to read short sections of more challenging books and academic journals – with practice these will become easier to understand.
- Understanding what commonly used words mean is not enough; you need to practise *using* these words accurately.
- Reflect and take action on the feedback your tutors give you to improve your written work.

Four points to note when learning a new word

Nearly all student word errors are due to one or more of the following: using a word that is nearly but not quite right; using the incorrect *form* (e.g. noun/adjective) of a word; getting words either side of the key word wrong; or making an error with the way the word fits into the rest of the sentence (the grammar).

So, when you learn a new word:

- Use your dictionary to find out whether the word can be used as:
  a noun – e.g. *Consideration* of this issue is important.
  a verb – e.g. We need to *consider* this issue carefully.
  an adjective – e.g. A *considerable* amount of research has been done on this issue.
  an adverb – e.g. We must conduct *considerably* more research in order to understand the effects of the drug.

- Take note of any common prefixes (such as *inter-*, *intra-*, *super-*, *anti-*, *poly-*, *post-*, *pre-*) which may help you understand a word and find out what the correct negative form of the word is. For example, the negative form of *appropriate* is <u>in</u>*appropriate* not <u>un</u>*appropriate*.

- Use your dictionary to find out whether the key word is often or always used with other specific words such as *in/at/on* or used in a particular phrase. For example:
  Consideration of this issue is vital.
  This issue is currently *under consideration by* the government.
  Careful consideration of this issue is important.
  We need to *take into consideration* the long-term effects.

- If the word is a noun, use your dictionary to find out whether it can be counted (i.e. can be both singular and plural) or is uncountable. For example:
  The word *consideration* can be counted. You can say 'There *is* one key *consideration*' or 'There *are several considerations* to take into account'.
  The word *research* cannot be counted. You can say 'important research has been conducted' but you cannot say '<u>*an*</u> important *research has* been conducted' or 'several important research<u>*es have*</u> been conducted'.

● Five techniques for using vocabulary and grammar to help you use your own words

Remember that when you paraphrase, just replacing individual words one by one from your source is not acceptable, and also that you should only be restating short sections of texts to show how they have informed your own ideas. A good paraphrase is your own reinterpretation of the text. However, there are some basic ways of using vocabulary and grammar to help you paraphrase (you can also use these techniques for summarising).

These are:

- using a different word that has the same meaning as the original word (a synonym);
- changing the form of the word;
- changing the tense of the verb;
- changing the structure of the sentence;
- changing the order of the information.

Below is a text extract and a good paraphrase of it from Section A5. Read the extract and the paraphrase and then look at the list which gives examples of how the five techniques above have been used.

Source extract

So far there is no clear evidence from health studies of a relation between mobile phone use and mortality or morbidity. Indeed, tantalising findings in humans include a speeding up of reaction time during exposure, particularly during behavioural tasks calling for attention and electrical brain activity changes during cognitive processes. It is not clear, however, whether these findings have any positive implications for health.

(Adapted from: Maier, M., Blakemore, C. and Koivisto, M. (2000) 'The health hazards of mobile phones'. *British Medical Journal*, 320 (7245), pp. 1288–1289.)

Paraphrase

Studies point to interesting results which suggest that mobile phone users experience quicker reaction times to some tasks which require both changes in electrical brain activity and concentration (Maier et al., 2000). Although it has not been shown that these effects represent actual benefits to health, there has equally been no data from any disease studies to suggest that mobile phones actually damage health in any way (ibid.).

Examples of the five techniques used to write the paraphrase

- Using synonyms

  tantalising findings changed to *interesting results*

  mortality and morbidity changed to *disease studies*

- Changing the word form

  mobile phone *use* (noun) changed to *using* (verb)

- Changing the tense of the verb

  there is no clear evidence of (present simple) changed to *there has been no data* (present perfect passive)

- Changing the structure of the sentence

  The student has put two points together in his last sentence and has used a sentence structure with *Although . . .* which was not in the original extract.

- Changing the order of the information

  The student has used the first point from the source (*no clear evidence*) as the last point in his paraphrase.

If you do not understand grammatical terms such as *verb* and *tense*, don't worry; you can use these techniques without knowing the grammatical labels. However, understanding basic grammatical terms is useful for developing vocabulary and for making full use of the information given in a dictionary. You will already have learnt some grammatical labels by reading this introduction, and the basic parts of speech are explained briefly in Section C4.

B1 Introducing your topic, aims and ideas

At the start of your essay you will probably need to introduce the topic, give some definitions and state the aims and limitations of your essay and then go on to introduce your
own points. Below are correct example sentences which use key words and phrases for
doing these things (you can also use these words for other functions in essays).
Alternative words or phrases and phrases with similar meanings are grouped together.

● Example sentences

Introducing the topic
1   The <u>fundamental</u>/<u>crucial</u>/<u>essential</u>/<u>main</u>/<u>most important</u>/<u>principal</u> environmen-
    tal <u>issue</u> is sustainability.
2   The <u>current</u> debate on/<u>controversy over</u> global warming <u>has received much atten-
    tion</u> in the media.
3   Blogs are a recent <u>phenomenon</u>.
4   The <u>question of whether</u> to legalise all drugs <u>is</u> <u>controversial</u>/<u>contentious</u>.
5   Targeted advertising is <u>the main factor in</u> the success of a business.
6   Cloning needs to be <u>viewed</u> <u>within the wider context of</u> genetic research.

Introducing definitions
1   E-technology <u>includes</u> mobile phones, computers and the internet.
2   The process <u>primarily</u>/<u>largely</u>/<u>mainly</u>/<u>generally</u> <u>consists of</u>/<u>comprises</u>/<u>involves</u>
    four <u>main</u>/<u>key</u> stages.
3   There are <u>numerous</u> but <u>similar</u> definitions of business ethics given by academic
    experts.
4   When describing what business ethics is, <u>it is essential</u> <u>to clarify</u> that it is not
    <u>synonymous with</u> the law or with morals in general.

Stating the aims of the essay
1   This essay will <u>address</u>/<u>consider</u>/<u>focus on</u>/<u>centre on</u>/<u>discuss</u>/<u>be concerned with</u>
    <u>the topic of</u>/<u>the subject of</u> relative poverty.
2   The <u>purpose</u>/<u>objective</u>/<u>aim</u>/<u>goal of this essay</u> is to <u>identify</u> solutions to the
    company's publicity problems.
3   <u>This essay will discuss</u> two main <u>elements</u> of organ transplantation.

THE MANCHESTER COLLEGE
COLLEGE LIBRARIES
ASHTON OLD ROAD
MANCHESTER
M11 2WH

| Introducing your topic, aims and ideas | 63 |

4 This essay will argue/propose that business ethics is essential to all companies.
5 I will discuss two different aspects of business ethics; as an area of study and as social practice.
6 This essay will focus/centre on the causes of poverty.

Stating the limitations of the essay

1 It is not possible/feasible to discuss all the issues in this essay.
2 It is not relevant/appropriate/pertinent to cover all areas/aspects of the debate in this essay.

Introducing your own point

Once you have introduced the topic and aims of your essay, you will need to introduce your own specific points and use your reading as evidence and support for these. Below are seven sentences which contain useful vocabulary for introducing your point. You should be able to identify what the content of the source following each sentence would be. (Answers are given in Appendix 7, p. 126.)

1 This concept/idea can be considered from several different viewpoints/perspectives.
2 There are two different views/opinions in this complex debate.
3 Misconceptions about cloning are widespread/prevalent.
4 There are diverse opinions as to whether ethics do have a valid place in a business.
5 One benefit/advantage of organic crops is that they do not use fertilisers or pesticides.
6 One drawback of/disadvantage of/problem with organic crops is that they produce a lower yield.
7 There is considerable research to show/prove that AIDS will be curable in the near future.

Moving from one point to another

1 Mobile phones have become an essential part of everyday life. As for/In regards to/Regarding potential health risks associated with mobile phones, such risks have yet to be proven.

● Notes on the use of some of these words

- ● *Involve* is used for a process, event or action.

- ● *Include* is used to describe some or most of the items in a set.

- ● *Compose* is used here in the passive tense (e.g. x is composed of y). The active tense (e.g. he composed the music) has a different meaning.

- *Element* has several different meanings. Usually it refers to a part or aspect of a whole.

- *Factor* usually refers to events, circumstances or influences which lead to a result.

- *View* as a noun (e.g. there are two views) has a similar meaning to *opinion*.

- *View* as a verb (e.g. we should view this as...) normally means 'to think about something in a particular way'. The nouns *viewpoint* and *perspective* also mean 'a way of thinking about something'.

Practice 10: Error correction

Below are 12 sentences from real student essays. The sentences are nearly but not quite right because the student has used the wrong word (given in italics). Replace these words with ones from the correct example sentences in this section. Use the form of the word (e.g. verb/noun/adjective) that fits correctly with the rest of the sentence. Answers are given on page 126.

1   The debate *constitutes of* three factors.
2   My essay will *consist of* the similarities and differences between the UK and American legal systems.
3   Another positive *concept of* organ transplantation is shorter waiting lists.
4   Overall, *in my perspective*, cloning is not a successful technique.
5   Thirdly, I will discuss the medical, ethical and scientific *concepts* of cloning.
6   Over the years, the *predicament* of whether GM food has a future has become increasingly important.
7   The report *involves* advice on how to increase profits.
8   According to Berk (1997) genetically engineered food has been *approached* into Britain's supermarkets.
9   In *modern* years the world wide web has become part of everyday life.
10 This essay will discuss the *topic* of whether violent films negatively affect children.
11 I will analyse this *debatable* issue from both a Marxist and a capitalist *opinion*.
12 The *thorough* use of pesticides in agriculture has led to contamination throughout the food chain.

Practice 11: Using your vocabulary to paraphrase

Below is a short text extract (note that it uses several key words given in this section). Read it, make brief notes and then paraphrase the extract. You should be able to use some of the vocabulary given in the example sentences in your paraphrase. Don't forget to use an in-essay reference. An example paraphrase is given in Appendix 7 on page 127.

Source extract

The widespread use of the sustainability concept testifies to the strength and relevance of its underlying themes for urban planning. Foremost among these themes is a concern for the long-term perspective. Though it seems only common sense that planning and building should be for the long-term, this is manifestly often not the case in practice.

(Adapted from: Wheeler, Stephen (1998) 'Planning Sustainable and Liveable Cities'. *The City Reader*, 3rd edition, R. T. Legates and F. Stout. London: Routledge (2003), p. 487.)

B2 Verbs for introducing and discussing your reading

This section provides you with key verbs (underlined) to use when reporting and discussing your reading and gives you important information on choosing appropriate reporting verbs.

● Three different ways of reporting your source

Below is an overview of the three different ways in which you can introduce or refer to a source.

The first method does not actually require a reporting verb but the second and third methods do.

1 Emphasising the information

If you wish to emphasise the idea or information in your source rather than the author, you should quote, paraphrase or summarise the information and only give the in-essay reference after the completed sentence in brackets (or as a number if you are using numeric referencing). For example:

> Although the law overlaps with ethics, it usually only regulates the lowest level of acceptable behaviour (Crane and Matten, 2007).

2 Emphasising both the information and the author

If you wish to emphasise both the information *and* the author of the source, you should refer in a general way to the fact that research or other work has been done, but again only give the specific reference towards the end of the sentence or in brackets after it. This emphasises both the information and the research or studies which have been done, rather than specific authors. This technique is useful for bringing together similar research or work and for referencing several authors as a group. Note that for this type of general reporting, the verb is usually used in the present perfect tense. For example:

> Research has indicated that job satisfaction is linked to regulating emotion (Côté and Morgan, 2002; Barrick, 2002).

You can also use the passive tense (with or without the 'by + agent' phrase). This also emphasises both the information and the authors.

> <u>It has been suggested that</u> watching violent films has a negative effect on children's behaviour (Carlton, 1999; Cyprian, 2001).

> <u>This idea</u> of the interdependence of any business organisation <u>is also supported by</u> Shaw and Barry (2007), Green (1994), Fritzsche (2005) and Svensson and Wood (2008).

3   Emphasising the author

To emphasise the specific author/s of the source, you should give the author as the grammatical subject of the sentence, with only the year of publication in brackets (or use a number for numeric referencing). You can also use this method when you want to show that you have reviewed the literature and that you know who the key authors are and which of them hold similar views to each other. For example:

> Svensson and Wood (2008) show that the two are in fact mutually dependent . . .

> Others such as Wolf (2008) share this view and Prindl and Prodham (1994) suggest that . . .

● Four key points to remember when using reporting verbs

Notice that for methods 2 and 3 above, you need to use reporting verbs to refer to your source, e.g. <u>indicate</u>, <u>suggest</u>, <u>support</u>, <u>show</u>. Below are four key points to remember when using reporting verbs.

1   Choose an appropriate verb

- Verbs commonly used to report what an author has done are ones such as: <u>establish</u>, <u>prove</u>, <u>show</u>, <u>demonstrate</u>, <u>investigate</u>, and <u>identify</u>. Make sure that you choose a verb which is correct for the object/noun; you can't <u>discover</u> an experiment or <u>argue</u> a question – you <u>conduct</u> an experiment and <u>address</u>, <u>discuss</u> or <u>examine</u> a question.

- Authors also often give their opinion in their text, so make sure that you also use a verb which reports this correctly. For example, if you want to express the fact that one author does not agree with something or someone, you would use verbs such as <u>question</u>, <u>query</u>, <u>challenge</u>, <u>dispute</u>, <u>reject</u> or <u>deny</u>. For example:

> Carr (1968) <u>challenges</u> the assumption that when managers talk about good ethics they are expressing a true desire to behave well.

- You can also use the reporting verb as a powerful opportunity to control your sources by showing *your* attitude to what the author says. For example, look at the sentence below from an article by Deborah Lupton (1998) entitled 'Medicine and health care in popular media'.

> Research would certainly suggest that the lay public has a strong interest in health and medical issues in the media.

If you want to agree with Lupton, you might report her in your essay using a 'positive' verb such as state, establish, show, demonstrate, note, inform, confirm, observe, point out or illustrate. For example:

> (i) Lupton (1998) shows that people are very interested in stories and news about medical and health matters.

However, if you wanted to argue against Lupton and say that the public does *not* have an interest in health and medicine in the media, you might report this reading in your essay using a 'negative' verb which implies that what the author says is questionable or wrong. Verbs commonly used to do this are claim, contend, maintain, or assert. For example:

> (ii) Lupton (1998) asserts that people are very interested in stories and news about medical and health matters.

Verbs such as argue, suggest, give, examine, use, describe, explain and discuss are more neutral and can be used to express either agreement or disagreement with your source.

2   Match your next sentence with the attitude of your reporting verb

Make sure that the attitude of your next sentence (positive, negative or neutral) is the same as that of the verb you have used to report your source. For example, which sentence below should follow each of sentences (i) and (ii) above?

(a) However, a large amount of media coverage given to such issues does not necessarily demonstrate that we are really interested in them.

(b) Indeed, some of the most popular current TV shows are hospital dramas.

3   Use the correct grammatical structure

In the active tense, all reporting verbs need to be followed by one of three structures:

(a) that + subject verb phrase
(b) what/why/where/who/whether + subject verb phrase
(c) a noun or object phrase

Some verbs can be followed by all three structures. For example:

(a) Lupton <u>shows that</u> the public is very interested in medical stories.
(b) Lin and Moon <u>show why</u> the public is very interested in medical stories.
(c) Research <u>shows</u> a link between folklore and history.

However, most verbs are commonly used with only one or two of these structures. Some verbs cannot be followed by *that* (e.g. *discuss*) and some cannot be followed by a noun phrase. Try to notice how reporting verbs are used. Your dictionary should help you identify the correct sentence structure for different verbs.

4   You may need more than one verb

Note that authors will often do more than one thing in their text and so you may often need two or more verbs. For example:

> Côté and Morgan <u>conducted</u> two studies and <u>demonstrated that</u> there is a link between regulating emotions and job satisfaction.

Practice 12: Error correction

Below are student sentences which contain errors in how the reporting verbs have been used. Sentences 1–9 use the wrong verb and sentences 10–12 use the correct verb but with the wrong grammatical structure.

1   Researchers in the UK are *undergoing studies about* the possible effects of the drug.
2   There is much evidence to *clarify* just how harmful cigarettes are.
3   Corson *imposed* that there are two main styles of English.
4   To summarise Karlov's argument, he *mentions* that playing chess uses a similar part of the brain to that used when playing music.
5   The idea of using a computer program to collectively edit a website was *perceived* by Cunningham and Beck in the late 1990s.
6   The telephone was *established* by Alexander Bell.
7   The ideas *portrayed* in the report are not new.
8   As *implied* by Murtaz (2007), 'patient care should be the primary motive for developments in the NHS' (p. 1).
9   Laurent (2007) *claims* that 'genetic engineering is the most important advance in medicine since the development of vaccines' (p. 15). This essay will demonstrate that this is clearly the case.
10   Lupton *discusses about* the portrayal of medicine and health in the media.
11   This essay will *argue a link* between regulating emotions and job satisfaction.
12   Emotion regulation is *defined that* you hide or try to modify your emotions.

B3 Describing cause and effect, change and data

There is a large amount of vocabulary for describing data and statistics and it is not possible to cover all of it here. This section gives example essay sentences which contain frequently used words and phrases for describing cause and effect and change from source information. Note that in many of the examples below, this key vocabulary has been used to reword sentences used in Part A.

● Example sentences

Discussing data and correlation

1 Côté and Morgan <u>showed from their data</u> that the amplification of pleasant emotions <u>happened more frequently than</u> the suppression of unpleasant emotions. <u>Importantly</u>, they also found <u>a strong correlation between</u> emotion regulation and job satisfaction and intention to quit. However, there was <u>no strong evidence to suggest</u> <u>an opposite correlation</u>, i.e. that job satisfaction and intention to quit influence emotional regulation.
2 There is <u>a direct link/correlation/causal link/direct relationship between</u> emotion regulation and job satisfaction (Côté and Morgan, 2002, cited in Robinson, 2008).
3 According to Svensson and Wood (2008), business and society are <u>mutually dependent/interdependent</u>.
4 It has been suggested that mobile phone use may be <u>associated with</u> quicker reaction times during exposure, <u>in conjunction with/together with</u> increased changes in brain electricity.

Cause, effect and consequences

1 Côté and Morgan demonstrated that as they <u>predicted</u>, the suppression of unpleasant emotions <u>leads to</u> <u>a decrease in</u> job satisfaction and therefore <u>an increase in</u> intention to quit.
2 People who amplify positive emotions at work have more positive social interactions. <u>Consequently,/As a result,/Therefore/Thus,</u> they have a higher level of job satisfaction.
3 It is important to note the direction of the correlation between job satisfaction and

emotion regulation; that job satisfaction <u>stems from</u>/<u>is due to</u>/<u>is a result of</u> job satisfaction.

4   The suppression of unpleasant emotions <u>leads to</u> a decrease in job satisfaction, <u>which in turn leads to</u> an increase in intention to quit. Their findings also suggest that an increase in the amplification of pleasant emotions will increase job satisfaction <u>through</u>/<u>via</u> positive social interaction with colleagues and customers.

5   One interesting study on emotion regulation has demonstrated that ability to regulate emotions at work <u>determines</u>/<u>is partially responsible for</u>/<u>can be attributed to</u>/<u>is a contributing factor to</u>/<u>is one cause of</u>/<u>is a major cause of</u> how satisfied we are with our job (Côté and Morgan, 2002, cited in Robinson, 2008).

6   <u>It is probable</u>/<u>likely</u>/<u>possible</u>/<u>almost certain</u> that emotion regulation <u>influences</u>/<u>affects</u> job satisfaction.

7   There is <u>a (strong) probability</u>/<u>likelihood</u>/<u>possibility</u> that emotion regulation influences job satisfaction.

8   Crane and Matten (2007) point out that the decisions businesspeople make can have significant <u>implications</u>/<u>consequences</u>/<u>effects</u>, yet managers often have no specific training in ethics.

Restricting, preventing and getting worse

1   Managers who only concern themselves with profit and ignore ethical perspectives can actually <u>hinder</u>/<u>restrict</u>/<u>limit</u> profitability.

2   Preventative drugs can <u>eliminate</u> the need for further treatment.

3   It has been suggested that the use of biometric data will <u>prevent</u> identification fraud.

4   An increase in financial instability will <u>exacerbate</u>/<u>worsen</u> the economic problems.

5   An increase in financial instability will lead to <u>a worsening of</u>/<u>an exacerbation of</u> the economic problems.

Helping and getting better

1   These findings <u>improve</u>/<u>enhance</u> our understanding.

2   An increase in sales and reduction in costs will <u>ameliorate</u>/<u>help</u> the company's problems.

3   Collins argues that a manager who takes into account business ethics will <u>facilitate</u> the success of the company.

Describing data and change

1   According to the 2008 report by the Government National Statistics Office, there has been <u>a steady rise</u>/<u>increase</u> in the UK natural population since 1901 with the exception of 1976 (no explanation is given for this <u>anomaly</u>).

2   There was <u>a sharp rise</u> in migration from abroad in 2005 but net migration <u>decreased</u> again in the following year. This <u>fluctuation</u> was probably due to

changes in immigration legislation. The overall population is increasing <u>at a constant rate of</u> about 0.5 per cent <u>per year</u> and the <u>trend</u> for the number of births to <u>outweigh</u> the number of deaths each year in the UK will continue for the foreseeable future (GNSO, 2008).

3 There was <u>a noticeable/significant/considerable decrease in the rate of</u> natural population growth until 2001–2, when the population started <u>to increase slightly</u> (GNSO, 2008).

4 The UK currently has an aging population, leading to <u>a decline</u> in <u>the proportion of</u> the people under 16 and an increasing proportion who are 65 or older (GNSO, 2008).

5 In 2006 <u>the average</u> age was 39.0 years and there has been only <u>a marginal/small/slight</u> increase <u>in</u> average age since then (GNSO, 2008).

6 <u>The majority of</u> immigrants are from the EU and only <u>a minority</u> are from African countries (GNSO, 2008).

Practice 13: Error correction

Below are student sentences which contain common vocabulary errors. You will be able to correct most of these sentences by using words and phrases from the examples given in this section.

1 Pollution is *enhancing* the problem of global warming.
2 There is commercial exploitation which *inflicts* people to sell their organs.
3 Pollution from new factories in China has *exaggerated* the problem of global warming.
4 The data *climaxes* the dangers of cannabis.
5 There is *a large* possibility that the experiment was flawed.
6 Profits have been rising *highly.*
7 Polio vaccinations in the 1960s had virtually *prevented* the disease by the end of the decade.
8 The data *infers* that lack of sunlight increases risk of depression.
9 An obvious *insinuation* of this data is that the drug is not effective.
10 As there is no firm evidence, we can only *predict* the cause of the population decline in 1976.
11 The research studies *ameliorate* our knowledge of sub-atomic particles.
12 The UK population is *generally* 60,000,000.
13 There was a *raise* in 2005 but in the *subsequent* year the figure fell to its previous level.

Practice 14: Summary

Below is an extract from the UK Government National Statistics report, 2008. Express the main points of information using your own words and vocabulary from this section and rephrasing statistics where possible.

There have been more births than deaths in the UK in every year since 1901, and as a result the population has grown due to natural change. In the year to mid-2006, births exceeded deaths by 159,000. This was the highest level of natural change since mid-1993. Until the mid-1990s, natural change was the main driver of population growth (UK Government National Statistics, 2008).

B4 Comparing the views of different authors

For most essays you will need to discuss different viewpoints on an issue or the advantages and disadvantages of something. You will therefore need to discuss your sources in relation to each other and state how the views of different authors are similar or different. Below are example sentences which give words and phrases for comparing sources with similar, different or diverging views and information, and for expressing contrast. In many of the example sentences the key vocabulary has been used to reword sentences from the business ethics essay and other text extracts used in Part A.

● **Example sentences**

Putting sources together that hold similar views

1   The Ethical Company Organisation emphasises the importance of business ethics and lists hundreds of companies. <u>Moreover</u>/<u>In addition</u>/<u>What is more</u>/ <u>Furthermore</u>, Crane and Matten (2007) state that the UK ethical market is valued at over 40 billion euros per year.
2   <u>Both</u> Wolf <u>and</u> Carr feel that businesses should not concern themselves with ethics.
3   Côté and Morgan (2002) <u>are in agreement with</u>/<u>agree with</u>/<u>share the same view as</u>/<u>hold a similar view to</u> Hochschild (1983), that emotion regulation can cause stress in workers.
4   Côté and Morgan (2002), <u>together with</u> Hochschild (1983), hold the view that emotion regulation may cause stress in workers.
5   <u>Neither</u> Wolf <u>nor</u> Carr feels that businesses should concern themselves with ethics.

Contrasting sources which hold opposite views

1   Writers such as Wolf (2008) argue that business should not concern itself with social consequences. <u>However</u>/<u>In contrast</u>/<u>On the other hand</u>, Svensson and Wood (2008) show that business and society are in fact mutually dependent.
2   Authors such as Wolf (2008) argue that business should not concern itself with

social consequences. Svensson and Wood, <u>however/on the other hand</u>, show that business and society are mutually dependent.

3   <u>Whereas/Although</u> Wolf (2008) believes that business should not concern itself with social consequences, Svensson and Wood (2008) show that business and society are mutually dependent.

4   Wolf (2008) believes that business should not concern itself with social consequences, <u>while/whereas</u> Svensson and Wood (2008) show that business and society are mutually dependent.

5   Wolf (2008) believes that business should not concern itself with social consequences. <u>Opponents of this view</u> such as Svensson and Wood (2008) suggest that business and society are mutually dependent.

Emphasising a point

1   Although the law overlaps with ethics, it usually only regulates the lowest level of acceptable behaviour (Crane and Matten, 2007). <u>In fact/Indeed</u>, business ethics is mainly concerned with issues and areas of business conduct which are *not* specifically covered by the law.

Diverging views and difference

1   Although Collins and Esty agree that businesses should be socially responsible, <u>their views differ in terms of/they diverge on</u> the extent to which businesses should be directly responsible for the effects of their production.

2   Collins' <u>view differs from that of</u> Esty <u>as to</u> the extent to which businesses should be directly responsible for the effects of their production.

3   There are <u>diverse/varied/different</u> opinions as to whether ethics do have a valid place in a business.

4   The literature reveals two <u>different/distinct/discrete</u> theories.

5   Côté and Morgan <u>differentiate/make clear the difference</u> between amplification and suppression of emotions.

But and *despite*

1   Crane and Matten point out that the decisions businesspeople make can have serious implications and consequences <u>yet/but</u> managers often have no specific training in ethics.

2   <u>Although</u> businesses need to be seen as ethical, the assumption cannot be made that they really are behaving in an ethical manner.

3   Businesses need to be seen as ethical <u>although</u> the assumption cannot be made that they really are behaving in an ethical manner.

4   We cannot assume that businesses behave in an ethical manner. <u>Nevertheless/Despite this/In spite of this/Still/However</u>, external pressures mean that businesses are being forced to act more ethically.

● Notes on the use of some words

● *Furthermore, moreover, however, in contrast, on the other hand, nevertheless, despite, in spite of* will usually start a new sentence (separated from the previous one with a full-stop or a semi-colon) and be followed by a comma.

● *Although, while, whereas* must be used to form a single sentence which has two clauses, not two separate sentences. These words can go at the start or in the middle of the sentence. If you use them at the start of a sentence, use a comma in the middle of the sentence to separate the two clauses.

● *Though* is similar to *although* but does have some subtle differences so it is safer to use *although*.

● *However* can be used to introduce an opposite and can also mean *despite this*.

● Remember to pay attention to the use of the various forms of words – e.g. *Difference*.

> *Difference* is a countable noun. For example, 'There is a difference/there are differences between ethics and morals.'

> *Different* is an adjective and must therefore be used with the verb *to be* (*is/are*) and a noun. For example, 'There are different issues.'

> *Differently* is an adverb and is used with a verb (e.g. *behave*). For example, 'Businesses should behave differently in the future.'

> *Differentiate* is a verb. For example, 'Côté and Morgan differentiate between amplification and suppression of emotions.'

Practice 15: Error correction

Below are real student sentences which have errors in how the vocabulary given above has been used.

1 Organic crops are expensive to buy (Miles, 2006). *However*, they are no healthier than non-organic crops (Smith, 2003).
2 There are a *distinct* range of languages spoken in London.
3 Côté and Morgan *contrast* between amplification and suppression of emotions.

4 Lewes (2000) argues that anyone can understand art. *Nevertheless*, Maitken disagrees and claims that for it to be fully understood, the viewer must know something about the history of art and about the artist.

5 *Although* there are several important advantages to parallel computing.

6 Treatment drugs for cancer are becoming much more effective. *In addition*, they still have significant side effects.

7 Neither Kibble *or* Price successfully demonstrates that the model works.

Practice 16: Comparing sources

Below are brief summaries of three different theories of job satisfaction. Imagine that these are your summaries and that you now wish to combine them into one paragraph which briefly compares the three theories. Write this paragraph using vocabulary from this section, rewording or reordering your summaries as necessary.

Summaries

1 Locke's theory states that what a person wants to do in a job (their 'conscious goals and intentions') and how far these goals are achieved, are the main factors which determine job satisfaction (Locke, 1968).

2 The dispositional approach sees a person's disposition as the most important element in determining their level of job satisfaction, regardless of the job type (Staw, Bell and Clausen, 1986).

3 The most complex model proposes that organisational structure influences the characteristics of a job, and that jobs with particular characteristics attract people with particular personality attributes. These attributes determine how satisfied a person will be with their job (Oldham and Hackman, 1981) and therefore both job type and employee personality are central to determining job satisfaction.

References

Locke, E. A. (1968) 'Towards a theory of task motivation and incentives'. *Organisational Behaviour and Human Performance*, 3 (2), pp. 157–89.

Oldham, G. and Hackman, J. (1981) 'Relationships between Organisational Structure and Employee Reactions: Comparing Alternative Frameworks'. *Administrative Science Quarterly*, 26 (1), pp. 66–83.

Staw, B., Bell, N. and Clausen, J. (1986) 'The Dispositional Approach to Job Attributes: A Lifetime Longitudinal Test'. *Administrative Science Quarterly*, 31 (1), pp. 56–77.

B5 Evaluating and discussing your reading

Evaluating and commenting on your reading is a fundamental part of an essay. As shown in section B2, the way you introduce a source and the reporting verb you choose will often give the reader an early indication of whether you agree with the source or not. For example, in the sentence below, the student introduces the source and uses the verb *give* in a positive way.

> Secondly, an even stronger argument for the view that good ethics in business do in fact exist, is that given by Collins (1994) and by other prominent experts on the subject.

However, you will usually also want to comment on your reading *after* you have described it. Below are some sentences that contain key words and phrases for doing this. If you are writing about your own experiment or data, you will still need to evaluate and comment on your results using this vocabulary.

● **Example sentences**

Positive comments

1   These findings are credible/valid/reliable/rigorous.
2   This argument is convincing/persuasive/powerful.
3   This data is complete/comprehensive.
4   Jones's approach is innovative because no one else has so far asked the question in this way.
5. This data is consistent with other research studies.
6   This clearly shows/indicates/demonstrates/proves the relevance of/the significance of/the importance of business ethics.
7   This research clearly suggests/shows that business ethics is important/significant/relevant.
8   Their model importantly demonstrates/shows that the ethical standards of society are also those of business.
9   This is clearly/manifestly/certainly an important step in furthering our understanding of this issue.

Positive comments but with some hesitation and distance

1   There is <u>perhaps/probably/possibly/arguably</u> a link between the two phenomena.
2   It <u>seems that/appears that/would seem that</u> personality does influence how we feel about our jobs.
3   These findings <u>suggest that/tend to suggest that/would tend to suggest that</u> our interest in TV hospital dramas is caused by our worries about personal safety.

Negative comments

1   There are <u>potential/possible</u> <u>problems with/errors in/flaws in</u> this theory.
2   This argument is <u>limited/flawed/unconvincing/unsatisfactory/of little importance</u> because <u>it does not take into account</u> all factors.
3   The study is <u>incomplete/inadequate</u> because it does not consider other models.
4   They <u>fail to</u> prove that this is the case.
5   Their proposition <u>lacks</u> concrete evidence. <u>There is a lack of</u> concrete evidence.
6   The research <u>ignores/does not take into account/fails to consider</u> the fact that other models also work.
7   There are <u>overt/explicit/clear</u> <u>problems with</u> the view that global warming does not exist.
8   There is <u>no solid reason/basis</u> for the research team's conclusion.
9   We should <u>disregard</u> this data because it is over 20 years old.

Phrases that can be used to introduce positive or negative comments

Below are a few phrases which could be followed by either a positive or a negative evaluation.

1   <u>Having considered/looked at/examined/analysed the results/the data/these findings/the debate, it would seem that</u> there is (not) a link between personality and job satisfaction.
2   <u>It is interesting/important/useful to note/to emphasise/to point out</u> that there does (not) seem to be a link.
3   <u>Interestingly/Importantly,</u> this evidence shows (does not show) that this view is correct.
4   <u>Clearly/It is clear that/It is evident that</u> this theory is correct (flawed).

Practice 17: Discussing a source

Below is part of the informal critical analysis on the article by Albert Carr on pages 122–123. Use this to write a more formal essay paragraph which comments on the article, using words and phrases from the example sentences above.

Extract from the critical analysis of the article by Carr

His style is quite persuasive – I instinctively feel he is partly right – but he is very cynical and oversimplifies. He gives no evidence for his views and doesn't try to be objective or look at opposing evidence. His argument isn't very well ordered as it is continuous opinion rather than a developed argument. I agree with Carr that some people feel they do need to lie in business but not that this is always the case or that business ethics are totally separate from social norms – not true nowadays?

B6 Informal words and phrases *not* to use

As explained in the introduction to Part B, you need to use a formal style in your essays that allows you to express complex ideas powerfully and precisely. Below are three key points which will help you use formal vocabulary and style.

● 1   Use nouns

Read the two paraphrases below. Both paraphrases give the same correct information (the results of the Côté and Morgan experiment) but in different writing styles.

Paraphrase 1
> Côté and Morgan did an experiment and they showed that people make or pretend to make themselves feel happier more often than when they try to hide feeling unhappy or angry. Another important thing they found out was that the way you hide or alter your feelings can have a big effect on how happy you are with your job, and whether or not you think you will leave it. However, they didn't find any evidence that people are affected the other way round, that how you feel about your job and leaving it affects how much you hide or change your emotions (Côté and Morgan, 2002, cited in Robinson, 2008).

Paraphrase 2
> Côté and Morgan showed from their data that the amplification of pleasant emotions happened more frequently than the suppression of unpleasant emotions. Importantly, they also found a strong correlation between emotion regulation and job satisfaction and intention to quit. However, there was no strong evidence to suggest an opposite correlation, i.e. that job satisfaction and intention to quit influence emotional regulation (Côté and Morgan, 2002, cited in Robinson, 2008).

Commentary on the paraphrases
Paraphrase 1 is written in a fairly informal style which uses lots of 'subject and verb' phrases (e.g. *people make, they try to hide, the way you hide, if you think, how you feel*). You may quite like this style and there is nothing grammatically incorrect about it; however, the constant use of *they/you* is too personal and also distracts the reader from the information being discussed.

Paraphrase 2 is written in a more formal style which uses more nouns (*amplification, emotions, suppression, correlation, job satisfaction, intention, emotional regulation*) instead of subject/verb phrases. This gives more emphasis to the information and makes the paraphrase more clear, concise and powerful.

● 2   Use one-word verbs

Avoid using two-word verbs such as *make up, get round, go up, help out* and *find out*. These types of verbs are too informal and often imprecise. Use a more formal one-word equivalent such as *compensate, avoid, increase, assist, investigate*. Phrases that use the verbs *get* and *go* (e.g. 'It's getting worse' 'it goes round in circles') are usually too informal for essays.

● 3   Avoid informal words and phrases

In paraphrase 1 above, the words *big* and *thing* were used. Such words are too informal and imprecise for essays. Table 3 gives some more words and phrases that students sometimes use in their essays but which are too informal for academic writing; do not use them.

Table 3 Informal words and phrases			
Imprecise, incomplete or lazy	**Too emotional, subjective or personal**	**Informal concluding phrases**	**Informal sayings**
etc.	terrible, incredible,	basically	in a nutshell
and so on	awful, pretty	it all comes down to	last but not least
thing	(meaning 'very')	at the end of the day	to put it mildly
stuff	obvious	after all	to name but a few
bit	really and truly	the thing is	no one is perfect
sort of	surely	along the way	
	everyone knows that	when it comes down to it	
	it's a great way of	anyway	
	it is so hard		
	it is such hard work		
	it is all too much		
	it's just not on		

Practice 18: Error correction

Below are real student sentences which contain informal words or
phrases. Correct or rewrite these sentences.

1   Globalisation is *very bad for* the planet.
2   Some companies behave unethically *and this kind of thing must stop.*
3   The issue will be *sorted* by the government.
4   *Basically,* there is no evidence that mobile phone use damages health.
5   *It all comes down to whether or not you can* regulate your emotions.
6   The dangers of cloning are *mind-boggling.*
7   *The point is,* companies need to pay more attention to business ethics.
8   Children who use drugs are often *left out in the dark.*
9   *The way this is going* there will not be adequate resources.
10 They were *bewildered* by the results.
11 Organ transplantation is *just* not effective.
12 Patients should not be treated *at all* like this.
13 We should *leave them alone.*
14 It will not help us *anyway.*
15 *It's a whole different ball game.*
16 The situation *can't go on like this.*
17 Globalisation can only lead to *the downfall of mankind.*
18 There are different kinds of businesses, private, public, non-profit
    making *etc.*
19 It's a *pretty big* problem.
20 The most important *thing to do* is to reduce carbon emissions.

Practice 19: Using a formal style

The paraphrase below is written in a style which is too informal.
Rewrite it in a more formal style, replacing the subject/verb phrases
with nouns where appropriate.

Paraphrase written in an informal style

Côté and Morgan showed that as they thought would happen, if you
keep a lid on bad feelings, you will be pretty unhappy with your job
and so you will be more likely to think about leaving it. Their results
also suggest that basically, if you increase your happy emotions,
you will feel better about your job because you will get on better at
work and you will get better responses from your workmates and
customers.

Part C Checking your work for mistakes

Introduction to Part C:
Why and how to check for mistakes

Making mistakes is a normal and positive part of the writing process, and making significant changes in the content and structure of your essay is also part of drafting and rewriting. An important stage in revising your draft is to make changes so that the essay makes sense to the person who will read it rather than just to yourself.

Part C focuses on the final stage of producing a good essay, which is 'polishing' and checking for grammatical errors. This is also an important part of the writing process. Many students would get much higher marks for their work if they checked it carefully for errors, not once but at least three times. Professional writers will often re-read their work at least seven or eight times.

The more you practise checking and correcting your work, the better you will become at it. Being able to edit your work is an important skill, not just for university study but also for your future employment. Some students do not realise just how important checking their CV and job application is; you should re-read your CV at least five or six times before sending it off. A CV sent to an employer which has more than a couple of small mistakes in it will usually be put straight in the bin.

● What Part C will do for you

Part C centres on common *grammatical* mistakes made in academic essays. The majority of mistakes students make involve only a small handful of grammatical areas. As an individual, you probably only make mistakes on two or three grammatical points, but if you keep making the same mistakes repeatedly in your essay, you may lose quite a few marks.

Part C sections give you:

- a brief explanation of grammatical points which are common sources of student error;
- real student sentences which contain common grammatical errors – nearly all the types of mistakes students make are covered in these sentences;
- the grammatical terms you may need, to help you find particular points in other books for further practice.

This book has taken you through the process of increasing your awareness, ability and confidence in knowing how to use your sources in your essays and in using relevant vocabulary. Part C completes this process by helping you improve your ability to check and correct your work.

Part C is not a complete grammar course and does not give detailed explanations of each point. The explanations given are intended as a revision and clarification of common problem areas; you may need to do some further work of your own if you have a real problem in a particular area. What Part C does give you is an awareness of the typical kinds of mistakes you might make and practice in spotting and correcting them. You will probably find some sections more useful than others, so use them as and when you need to.

● A strategy for checking your work

Make sure you leave enough time for checking your work. Once you have finished writing your essay, put it away for at least a few hours if you can – the longer the better. Then print out your essay and check this paper version rather than checking your work on screen. Reading a paper version helps you to see your essay in a fresh and more objective way, almost as someone else's piece of work and you will spot mistakes much more easily. Importantly, it will help you to see what you have really written, rather than what you *think* you have written. Reading a paper version of your work slowly out loud is an effective way of seeing what you have actually written and of hearing mistakes you might not detect just by reading your work in your mind. When you have corrected the mistakes you find, print and read your essay out again. Remember that the grammar and spell check on your computer will only detect a very limited range of mistakes and that it is not a substitute for careful checking and editing.

C1 Ten common grammatical mistakes

Below are brief explanations of the ten grammatical areas that students find the most problematic and which cause the majority of errors in student writing. Each point is followed by student sentences which contain errors (these errors are *not* highlighted) for you to correct.

1   *Important* or *importance*?
As stated in Part B, you need to make sure that you use the correct form of a word. Definitions and examples of the basic word forms are given below. Your dictionary will also give you the different forms of a word.

noun – a place, person or thing, e.g. *an article, a book, an essay title, research.* Many nouns used in essays are things you can't actually touch or see, e.g. *an issue, a theory, a problem, a debate, an argument, a discussion, an assumption, an increase, a conclusion, importance, relevance, consideration.*

adjective – describes a noun, e.g. a *long* article, *rigorous* research, a *controversial* debate, a *flawed* assumption, a *clear* conclusion, a *relevant* model, a *problematic* issue, *conclusive* results, a *considerable* amount of research.

verb – an action, e.g. *to argue, to show, to increase, to debate, to discuss, to theorise, to problematise, to conclude, to imply, to consider;* or a state, e.g. 'I am', 'I have'.

adverb – usually describes a verb (adverbs can also describe an adjective or another adverb) and often ends in *-ly*, e.g. It is *arguably* the most important issue. It *conclusively* shows that the drugs are ineffective. This view has been *positively* demonstrated. The rate has increased *considerably.*

Note that different word forms may sometimes have slightly different meanings. For example, *a conclusion* means 'the end of something'. However, *conclusive* and *conclusively* mean 'definite' or 'definitely'.

Practice 20: Error correction

1 Knowles (2000) difference between the theory and practice of
   primary education.
2 The population rose by three percentage a year.
3 Countries are making changes to suit tourisms.
4 The process has advantageous.
5 The process continuous to the final stage.
6 This has made a great contributing to society.
7 The article clear states that more research needs to be conducted.
8 Some people have strong religion believes.
9 A vital factor in counselling is trust and confident.
10 Conclusively, this essay has shown that this question needs further
   investigation.
11 The main negative factors in organ transplantation are the expense
   of the operation, the length of waiting time and risking your health.
12 There is still a potentially market.

2   *Have* or *has*?

In your essays you will often need to use the singular subject *he, she, it*, or an equivalent such as *Smith/the software/the experiment/the research/this essay*. This is called
the third person singular.

With the third person singular, regular verbs in the present tense use verb + *s*, the
verb *to be* uses *is/has been/was* and the verb *to have* uses *has/has had/had*.

> Smith shows.
> The experiment is flawed.
> This journal has credibility.

Using + *s* with the verb for the third person singular causes understandable confusion
in student writing, because we usually associate an *s* with plurals. However, in English
it is the subject or object which indicates a plural, *not* the verb. For example:

> Plural subjects: They are correct.
>   The articles are reliable.
> Plural objects: I have three essays.
>   There were two experiments.

So, you need to remember the strange rule that the plural subjects *you/we/they* do *not*
use verb + *s* but that the third person singular *does* use verb + *s*.

Table 4 The third person singular verb form	
Third person singular subject +	**Verb**
he/she/it/Smith/the book/the article/ the experiment/the research team/ the author/the theory/the issue/the debate/the data	Present tense regular verbs: *shows/reports/involves/increases/concludes*
	To be: *is/was/has been* To have: *has/had/has had*

● **Uncountable nouns**

Some important nouns cannot be used on their own as a plural and are only used in the third person singular. Examples of these words are those which refer to academic disciplines, for example, *genetics, mathematics, science* and words such as *research, equipment, progress, information, evidence, proof, importance, relevance, significance.* For example:

> The research shows that
> Equipment is expensive.
> Progress has been made.
> The information was useful.

● **Common phrases which use the third person singular verb form**

There is much evidence to suggest
There is little proof that
It is either the first or the second solution which has contaminated the slides.
Neither Wolf nor Carr feels that businesses should concern themselves with ethics.
Everyone/anyone/someone/no one understands that
Another problem is
The (total) number of cases is not significant.
The average age is
A large/small/significant amount of work has been done on this topic.

Table 5 The plural subject verb form	
Plural subjects: we/they/you +	**Verb**
The books/ the authors/the issues/ the results/the research projects	Present tense regular verbs: *show/report/ involve/increase/conclude*
	To be: *are/were/have been* To have: *have/had/have had*

- **Common phrases that can use the third person singular or plural verb form**

There are many projects . . ./There are few studies . . .
Other issues include the expense and the health risks.
A (large/small/significant) number of patients have recovered.

- **Countable nouns**

Countable nouns can be used in the third person singular (verb + s) or as a plural subject (verb without s), e.g. *researcher, project, statistic, study, experiment, theory, findings, essay*. For example:

The researcher has shown that . . . OR The researchers have shown that . . .
The research project involves . . .   OR The research projects involve_ . . .

- **Common phrases that can use the third person singular or plural verb form**

If the first noun in the sentence is a fraction, percentage or proportion, the verb should agree with the noun closest to it and so the verb can use the third person singular or the plural form. For example:

The majority/a minority/60%/two-thirds/a quarter of the respondents/the essays are incorrect.
The majority/60%/two-thirds/a quarter of the population/the essay is incorrect.

Practice 21: Error correction

1 The number of tourists have increased.
2 Smith et al. (2000) reports that this level of violence is harmful.
3 Recent research also show that the drugs are effective.
4 The stress response help the body to react.
5 Malicious software such as worms have been increasingly used.
6 The two types differs in the way they can be treated.
7 A research company have recently produced a new report.
8 Kline imply that ethics is not important.
9 The use of mobile phones have long-term effects.
10 Many research are carried out in laboratories.
11 A large amount of water are reabsorbed in the colon.
12 One of the main differences are the weight.
13 Many information can be collected via the questionnaires.

3   Sentence structure
Missing verbs
Don't forget that all full sentences must contain at least one verb.

Practice 22: Error correction

1   For example, the risk to the health of the patients.
2   Firstly, the positive aspects of drug therapy.

Missing clauses
A clause is a word group that has at least a subject and a verb. Some clauses cannot stand alone as a complete sentence. A clause that begins with a word such as *although*, *because*, *since*, *if*, *unless* and *until* must be followed by a **second clause** to be a sentence. Similarly, clauses starting with *which*, *that* or *who* must be followed by a **second clause** which has a verb.

Practice 23: Error correction

3   Although there are several advantages.
4   Our data, which shows a direct correlation between lack of light and depression.

Missing *that*
A common error is to miss out *that* after some reporting verbs + clause.

Practice 24: Error correction

5   Dorkin argues if people want to eliminate poverty, taxes must be increased.
6   Herschel points out the theory of relativity is difficult to understand fully.
7   Donne states the experiment was a success in terms of raising further questions for study.

Too many clauses in one sentence
If a sentence is too long, with too many clauses, it will be unclear and very difficult to read. Sentences should usually have not more than two clauses and a maximum of three clauses. If you put together two clauses which could both stand alone as

complete sentences, it is not enough to separate them with just a comma. You should either split them into two separate sentences or use an appropriate co-ordinating word: *and, yet, or, so, for, nor*.

Practice 25: Error correction

8   Côté and Morgan have shown that emotion regulation influences job satisfaction and that amplifying positive emotions increases positive interaction with both colleagues and customers, but that there is not an opposite correlation, that is, that job satisfaction affects emotion regulation.
9   The business decisions managers take can have significant implications, most managers do not have training in business ethics.
10   The worldwide web is a constantly developing technology, it has many advantages for society.

4   *In, at* or *on*?

Prepositions (e.g. *in, at, on, over, for, with*) give the relationship between a verb and a noun. It is important to use the correct preposition, as different prepositions can give very different meanings. For example:

research <u>on</u> nuclear physics
research <u>by</u> Jones
research <u>for</u> the government
research <u>under</u> Dr Patel
research <u>at</u> the hospital

Some words only ever use one specific preposition; your dictionary should tell you which preposition to use with a word.

Practice 26: Error correction

1   (Patel, 2000, cited from Bragg, 2003)
2   Deforestation does not only have significant effects within one part of the world.
3   I will discuss about violence in computer games.
4   Diabetes can be broken down in two types.
5   Prevention for type one diabetes is not possible.

6   A conclusion will be drawn on whether ethics is important to business.

7   They all contribute in to making an improvement to the environment.

8   They are both at a constant state of balance.

9   There are negative effects on non-organic crops, such as a reduction in biodiversity.

10   The materials used were pertinent of the experiment.

11   One of the similarities of online and paper sources is that both forms have been written by someone.

12   In an Islamic perspective, therapeutic cloning is permissible.

5   *To find* or *finding*?

Some phrases use *to* + verb (the infinitive) and some phrases use a preposition followed by the verb in the '-ing' form. For example:

Infinitive:	the <u>failure to accept</u>
	they <u>neglect to show</u>
	they <u>expect to find</u>
	we <u>attempt to prove</u>
Preposition + [verb]-ing:	the <u>process of filtering</u>
	the <u>success in solving</u>

Practice 27: Error correction

1   The model is capable to make accurate predictions.

2   The increase in greenhouse gases is caused by the cut down of trees on a large scale.

3   The process to utilise the waste products is complicated.

4   The failure of cells from removing sugars causes diabetes.

5   Lewes (2000) rejects the idea to use DNA as evidence of guilt.

6   *The* or nothing?

A common mistake in student writing is to miss out *the* (called the 'definite article') or to use it where there should be nothing. The use of articles is quite complicated but below is a reminder of when to use *the* and when there should be no article.

No article

●	Non-specific singular nouns:	Some groups in society object to this law.
●	Non-specific uncountable nouns:	Research into cancer has increased. Progress has been made in cancer treatment. You need evidence to support a claim.
●	Non-specific plural nouns:	People are complex. Experiments need to be reliable. Articles in academic journals are useful.
●	Most proper nouns (names) including their possessive form:	Smith, Einstein, Freud Smith's research, Einstein's theory, Freud's idea.

The

●	Specific singular nouns (usually with *of*):	The society of today The people of France The analysis of the data The author's opinion The study's conclusion The theory of chaos The experiment on the virus The liquid in the test tube
●	Specific uncountable nouns:	The research at the Bonn Institute is important. The progress made by Smith's team is remarkable. The evidence used to support your claim is not adequate.
●	Specific plural nouns:	The people at the conference The experiments mentioned earlier in the report The articles used in the essay
●	When only one exists:	The nuclear transfer method The immune system The organic method
●	Ordinals:	the first, the second, the last
●	Superlatives:	the least, the most, the best, the highest, the most recent
●	Specifiers:	the main factor, the principal issue, the essential question, the only/the same report
●	Part of a whole:	none of the, all of the, some of the, most of the, half of the
●	Names used as adjectives:	the Freudian theory of psychosis.

Practice 28: Error correction

The sentences below either have *the* where there should be nothing, or have nothing where there should be *the*.

1 There are some groups among the society which object to this research.
2 It is expected that public will benefit from this technology.
3 Researchers at University of North Texas have discovered a new drug.
4 Cloning is a controversial issue in the society.
5 Carbon dioxide mostly comes from burning of coal and other fossil fuels.
6 Third disadvantage is that it is expensive.
7 The impact of this legislation in UK has been profound.
8 For majority of people, mobile phones are now almost indispensable.
9 Author's position is neutral on this question.
10 The deforestation of Amazon Basin could lead to an increase in global temperature.
11 The study shows that immune system is extremely complex.
12 Exam timetable did not indicate what time exam was going to start.

7 Commas with *that*

Students sometimes use commas with *that* where there should not be a comma. Nearly all sentences and phrases with *that* do <u>not</u> have commas.

- ### *that* – no comma

The evidence suggests that . . .
It seems/appears/is clear that . . .
It is likely/probable that . . .
It is important that we consider . . .
The fact is that . . .
The results were published so quickly that the newspapers . . .
The same research team that discovered the virus has now produced an effective vaccine.
The experiment that was conducted by Smith's team provided useful data.

- ### *that* + comma

There is only one *that* phrase which uses commas. This is the phrase *that is* (meaning 'namely') used before a dependent clause. When you use <u>that is</u> you need a comma before and after these two words. For example:

> There is one key issue, <u>that is</u>, the consequences for the environment.

Practice 29: Error correction

1   It has been shown in this essay that, this is not the case.
2   It is illogical, that people think pollution is not important.
3   The fact is that, we cannot determine the outcome.
4   This essay will discuss the most important aspect of genetic research that is cloning.

8   Commas with *which*

Essential information clauses – no commas
If the *which/who* . . . part of your sentence is essential information, do not use commas. In the two examples below, the underlined part of the sentence is essential to show which experiment and which authors are being discussed.

> The experiment <u>which was conducted by Smith's team</u> provided useful data but Mitchell's experiment did not.

> Authors <u>who disagree with Carr</u> include Esty and Collins.

NB   It is clearer and more correct if you use *that* in essential information clauses rather than *which* or *who* (so again, phrases with *that* do not have a comma). For example:

> The experiment <u>that was conducted by Smith's team</u> provided useful data but Mitchell's experiment did not.

Extra information clauses – two commas
If the *which/who* . . . part of your sentence is additional information (and could be left out of the sentence) rather than essential information, use a comma each side of this clause.

In the examples below, the underlined part is *not* necessary to show what or who is being discussed.

> Business ethics, <u>which has become increasingly important</u>, can be defined as principles of behaviour as applied to business organisations.

> Svennson and wood, <u>who disagree with Carr</u>, propose a dynamic model of business ethics.

Practice 30: Error correction

1 Many commentators have suggested that a system, which allows different states to have autonomy would be best.
2 There are many factors, which may affect the way a text is written.
3 Patel's data which was collected from over 300 questionnaires, showed that our proposition was correct.
4 The data, which was collected by the first research team proved not to be as reliable as that collected in later studies.

9   Apostrophes

You should not use contractions in formal writing (do not = don't, they are = they're, it is/has = it's, who is = who's, that woman is = that woman's) so there should only be one reason to use an apostrophe in your essays: to show possession.

Remember that you only use an apostrophe to show possession; never use an apostrophe to indicate a plural. For example:

Possession: Research teams from this country**'s** scientific community developed the drug

Plural: Research teams from seven countr**ies** developed the drug.

Apostrophe to show possession
Look at the examples below.

The study <u>of Smith</u> = <u>Smith</u>**'s** study
The economy <u>of a country</u> = a <u>country</u>**'s** economy
The article <u>of Jones</u> = (Jone**s's** article) = <u>Jones</u>**'** article

Note that in the third example, the apostrophe still comes after the noun (Jones) as normal but because *Jones* ends with an *s* the possessive *s* is sometimes written down because *s's* is thought to look confusing. For the same reason, plural nouns that end with *s* do not use the second possessive *s*. For example:

Reports from rich countri**es**   = (Rich countrie**s's** reports)   = Rich countrie**s'** reports

The data of the researcher**s**   = (The researcher**s's** data)   = The researcher**s'** data

If the noun is plural but does not end with an *s* use both the apostrophe and the possessive *s* as normal. For example:

The attitude of some people   = Some people**'s** attitude
The experience of the children = The children**'s** experience

Its or *it's*?

Students often make the mistake of using *it's* to show possession where there should be no apostrophe. A correct example is given below.

The title of the article is 'Expression' = <u>Its</u> title is 'Expression'.

Incorrectly using *it's* is an understandable mistake because of the use of the apostrophe for possessive nouns, as shown above. Also, words such as *anyone's, anybody's, someone's* and *one's* do use apostrophes. However, the possessive personal *pronouns mine, yours, his, hers, its, ours, theirs* do not use an apostrophe.

Remember that *it's* with an apostrophe is only used for the contraction of *it is* or *it has* and is too informal for essay writing, so you should never need to use *it's* in an essay.

Practice 31: Error correction

1 Some theologist's think that therapeutic cloning is acceptable.
2 Greenpeace states that one of it's aims is to expose threats to the environment.
3 A countries government usually resides in the capital city.
4 An employees career depends on many different factors.
5 The issue of who's concerns are most important is still unresolved.
6 People should look after their bodies health.
7 The experiment's were conducted with rigour.
8 The article does not discuss the issue in detail. It's main proposition is that the womens movement in the 1960's to 1980's was not as effective as is often thought.
9 Employee's need to wear clothes which are appropriate for this type of work.
10 The researcher's data shows that they have not proved a direct correlation.

10 Direct and indirect questions

Students often make one of the three following mistakes with direct or indirect questions:

- Using too many direct questions.

Direct questions are a little too informal for academic writing, so only use them occasionally.

- Using an indirect question with the word order of a direct question. Indirect questions have an introductory phrase which indicates that we are questioning something, and then a second clause which has the same word order as for a non-question statement.
- Using a question mark with an indirect question – an indirect question uses a full-stop.

Table 6   Direct and indirect questions

Direct question	Indirect question
<u>What is</u> the key issue in global warming?	We need to ask/consider/It is unclear <u>what</u> the key issue in global warming <u>is</u>.
<u>Can</u> mobile phones <u>cause</u> illness?	The question is/We need to ask whether the use of mobile phones <u>can cause</u> illness.
<u>What has</u> this research <u>achieved</u>?	It is unclear/We need to ask/The question remains as to what this research <u>has achieved</u>.

Practice 32: Error correction

1   The question is whether mobile phones make us sick?
2   The issue is if this will lead to an increase in violence.
3   Research was conducted to see what was the cause of the disease.
4   It is unclear what is the key issue in global warming.
5   The question remains as to what has this research achieved.

C2 Mistakes with in-essay references

Mistakes with in-essay references

Below are student sentences which contain mistakes in how the student has referred to the source or author in their essay. The errors are *not* highlighted. Identify the mistake or mistakes in each sentence and correct them.

Practice 33: Error correction

1. According to (Dr Reynolds, 2000) there is no strong evidence of long-term damage to health.
2. According to Dr Padash 2000 there is no strong evidence of long-term damage to health.
3. George Marchais (1984) discusses three main factors.
4. Locke (97) suggests that we need more evidence.
5. 'Global warming is a factual truth' (Greenpeace article).
6. The website has drawn attention to the fact that more research needs to be done.
7. A strong economy relies on moderate taxation methods (Sloman, *Economics*, 3rd Edition).
8. These factors can be seen in the article titled 'Biometric data of the future'.
9. 'Locke and Himenez' show that early pre-school learning improves children's ability to process information.
10. Smoking and related illness causes over 500,000 deaths annually in the UK.
11. **Folour and Skipton** (1991) found a strong correlation between amount of exposure to sunlight and depression.
12. Smith's article entitled location and personal identity, demonstrates how closely the two are related.

Mistakes with using words such as *according to, quote, cite* or *source*

When you quote or paraphrase a source, you should not actually use the words *quote* or *cite* unless you are stating that one author has cited or quoted another author. You should not talk about the process you went through of researching and reading sources for your essay, unless you are specifically asked to do so.

Practice 34: Error correction

1 According to me, the issue of global warming is not as serious as the media portrays.

2 Kerlinger (1969) quotes that '*Science* is a misused and misunderstood word' (p. 1127).

3 From the published book written by Jones (2002) we can see that governments need to address this issue urgently.

4 As Collins (1994) cites, 'good ethics is synonymous with good management' (p. 2).

5 These factors are discussed in the source 'Dying to be thin'.

6 After researching many sources and reading eight articles over the last two weeks, I have found that the issue of global warming is controversial.

Mistakes with sentence grammar

Points to note are:

- if you use the author or article as the subject of your sentence, you should not also use words such as *it* or *they/their research*;
- if you use the structure '*As* Smith *states/shows/demonstrates* . . .' do not use *that* after the verb.

Practice 35: Error correction

1 Côté and Morgan (1999) their research showed that emotion regulation affects job satisfaction.

2 Coates and Bailey (1995) their study examined three main aspects of mental health.

3 According to the New Scientist (8/1/2005), it states that people are still not aware of the effects the use of mobile phones can have.

4 As Crème and Lea (1997) stated, that the gap between academic and personal writing is not as far apart as we assume.

5 According to Smith (2000) states that the problem is widespread.

Mistakes with grammar and punctuation when using quotations

Practice 36: Error correction

1 In addition to this, 'effects on memory and attention and how microwaves alter electrical activity on the brain' will also be studied'. (New Scientist (2005))

2 Knowles (1998) 'It has to be stated that groups work more efficiently' (p. 64).

3 Jones 2006 'importance of understanding the causes of mental ill health' (p. 12).

C3 Being too general or unclear

Below are student sentences which contain the type of errors specified under each heading. Decide what is wrong with each sentence and then read the commentary and answers in Appendix 7.

Overgeneralisation, unspecific or unsupported statements

1   Women are better than men.
2   Millions of women risk their lives to stop unwanted pregnancy.
3   The majority of men gamble in their twenties.
4   There are hundreds of women attacked each year.
5   Everyone knows that drugs are addictive.
6   There is more demand for organ transplants than ever before.
7   The UK has an increasing number of drug users.
8   We all see writing as being the same but there are different writing forms and functions.

Not explaining yourself clearly

1   The Mediterranean which is the dirtiest sea in the world is caused by tourism.
2   I have chosen to discuss cloning because I want to put forward the major advance technology and why I consider cloning to be prohibited.
3   Cloning animals has been debated between scientists, politicians and the general public on how cloning has been treated and how they might clone humans.
4   The nephron has five main parts for the process to work.
5   Academic writing is a form of writing that students adapt to their work.
6   Personal writing is more of your own feelings.
7   This is a holiday development for the country.
8   Deoxygenated blood is pumped from the heart into the lungs and vice versa.
9   Luchens (2006) found that some children are allowed to watch violent films by their parents and that they behave more aggressively after watching them.

C4 Missing words and extra words

Below are student sentences which contain the type of errors specified under the relevant heading. Correct each sentence.

Missing words or phrases

1 When deforestation, the earth's ability decreases and cannot remove carbon dioxide.
2 A good dictionary is to find out the meaning of a word.
3 'Cultural baggage' is tourists carrying their own values.
4 For example, the correlation between diet and disease.
5 The process continues to the final stage which in the second coiled tubule.
6 Organ transplantation has risks involving the rejection of the immune system.
7 Some consider homosexuality to be morally wrong and should therefore be classified as illegal.
8 Research shows that by regulating your emotions, for example pretending to be happier than you are.
9 In this case we have to search each word that we do not know, at least a rough meaning.
10 Is clear from this data that further studies need to be conducted.

Extra words

1 Although there are many differences between formal and informal writing.
2 This essay will examine how businesses are run, bearing in mind with the ethical issues.
3 Type two diabetes it can be managed by having a healthy diet and lifestyle.

Wrong phrase order

1 Animal testing has been disputed, whether it is right or wrong.
2 There is a natural connection between spoken language and the cultural identity of a group, for example the accent, vocabulary and discourse patterns.

Appendix 1
Glossary and definitions of terms used

Abstract a summary (usually of about 100 words) of an article, report or book, which includes the main argument or problem, the procedures, results and conclusion. Abstracts are always written by the authors of the source and are normally used by readers to decide whether they want to read the whole text.

Academic/scholarly journal a journal which contains reliable, peer-reviewed articles of good quality.

Academic source a book, article or other type of text which has been peer-reviewed and/or is written by experts in the subject.

Argument a sequence of reasons to support a particular theory or point of view.

Bibliographic details the full details of a source, given at the end of a written text.

Citation information on who wrote something, given within the piece of writing. *Citation* is also sometimes used to mean a quotation.

Close paraphrase when most of the words of the original source are used with only small changes. Close paraphrase should only be used when taking notes.

Critical analysis/thought the process of identifying the argument of a text and then questioning and evaluating it to decide whether it is based on correct assumptions, logical reasoning and sound evidence.

Digest a brief summary of one source or a compilation of summaries of many different sources on a particular topic. It can be written by the authors themselves or by a third party.

Draft a rough version of an essay or other piece of written work, which is changed and improved to produce the finished piece.

et al. abbreviation of the latin *et alii* meaning 'and others'. Used for in-essay referencing when a source has more than two authors.

Evaluation, to evaluate to reflect on and assess the information and argument of something.

Extract a section of text.

ibid. from the latin *ibidem* meaning 'in the same place'. Used as an in-essay reference to indicate that the source is exactly the same as the one previously given.

i.e. from the latin *id est*, meaning 'that is'. In writing, *i.e.* is used to mean 'that is to say' or 'in other words'. Be careful not to confuse *i.e.* with *e.g.* With *i.e.* you must restate the complete idea or complete set of items. With *e.g.* you only give one or two examples of the set.

Literature review   summarising and comparing the key authors and sources on a particular topic or issue.

Literature search   the process of looking for, finding and selecting relevant material and sources.

Paraphrase, to paraphrase   re-expressing all the information and ideas from a section of text in your own words and style.

Peer-review   the system by which articles are checked for quality and accuracy by relevant academic experts before being published.

Plagiarism, to plagiarise   presenting someone else's ideas, information, wording or style (or any combination of these) as your own, even if it is only a single sentence. Plagiarism also includes claiming that work done jointly with other students is solely your own work (this is called 'collusion'). Plagiarism can occur accidentally due to poor writing and referencing, or on purpose to gain a particular advantage or benefit.

Primary source   the first, original source of information or ideas, for example the original report written by the person who conducted an experiment or the original article or book written by an author.

Quotation, to quote   a phrase, sentence or section of a source given in your writing, word for word, without any changes in wording from the original text.

Research   any type of organised search, study, investigation or work that is done in order to develop ideas and knowledge.

Scan   to look at or read something quickly in order to identify key points or to assess whether something is relevant for more detailed reading.

School of thought   a way of thinking, set of beliefs, or accepted theory or approach, e.g. behaviourism, socialism, Marxism, feminism.

Secondary source   a source which writes about, discusses or uses a previously written primary source.

Text   a word used to describe any type of written document when focusing on the content rather than the type of document.

Appendix 2
Dictionary entry and explanation of abbreviations

Example of a dictionary entry

consider. v. 1. think carefully about or believe to be. 2. Look attentively at.
- phrases **all things considered** – taking everything into account.

considerable. adj. 1. notably large. 2. having merit or distinction.
- DERIVATIVES **considerably** adv.

consideration. n. 1. careful thought or fact taken into account when making a decision.
- phrases – **in consideration of** in return for. **take into consideration** take into account. **under consideration** being considered.

considering. prep and conj. taking into consideration.

(Adapted from: Pearsall, J. (ed.) (1999) *Concise Oxford Dictionary* (10th edn). New York: Oxford University Press.)

Common abbreviations used in dictionary entries

n.	=	noun
adj.	=	adjective
v.	=	verb
adv.	=	adverb
prep.	=	preposition
conj.	=	conjunction (a word that joins two clauses)
sing.	=	a singular noun/treated as singular, e.g. **genetics is** an interesting field of study.
pl.	=	plural noun, e.g. **children are** important.
mod.	=	modifier (a noun used as an adjective to modify a second noun), e.g. a **family** reunion).
usu.	=	usually used as

Register labels used in dictionary entries

The word *register*, when referring to language, means the commonly accepted style and level of formality of language used in a particular context, e.g. a medical register.

Register labels which indicate that the word is suitable to use in an essay are:

form/formal and *technical.*

If no register label is given for a word, it is probably suitable to use in an essay. Register labels which indicate that the word is <u>not</u> suitable for essays are:

informal/inf., dated, archaic, poetic/literary, rare, humorous, euphemistic, dialect, offensive, vulgar, slang, derogatory.

Appendix 3
Commonly confused words

Below are pairs of words which students sometimes confuse, given with correct example sentences. If you often confuse two similar words, look up each word in a dictionary and practise using them correctly.

- **Words with completely different meanings**.

accept – v. / *except* – prep. and conj.
  Businesses need to **accept** that ethics are central to success.
  All the trials **except** the study by Roshier indicate that the drug is effective.

ensure – v. / *insure* – v.
  We must **ensure** that the equipment has been rigorously tested.
  The business was **insured** against fire for £3 million.

lose – v. / *loose* – adj.
  Despite the clear benefits, we should not **lose** sight of the fact that organ transplantation carries significant risk to the patient.
  The rope that secured the boat became **loose**.

past – adj., n., prep. / *passed* – v. (from the verb *to pass*)
  I went **past** the shop. (preposition – not commonly used in essays)
  In **past** decades, few members of the public knew the meaning of the term *genetics*.
  The government **passed** the new law last week. The new drug has successfully **passed** initial trials.

precede – v. / *proceed* – v.
  Darwin's theory of evolution **preceded** the theory of modern evolutionary synthesis by about a century.
  After collecting the cells, we **proceeded** to examine them under a microscope.

principal – adj. / *principle* – n.
  The **principal** aim of this essay is to examine the importance of business ethics.
  Business ethics can be defined as the **principles** of good and bad behaviour as applied to business.

to – prep. / *too* – adv.
  There is **too much** work **to** do for one person.

- **Different word forms with similar meanings**

advice – n. / *advise* – v. (NB   advise needs a **s**ubject)

The **advice** given in the report was useful.

The company **advised** all its customers to return the toys as soon as possible.

effect – n. / *affect* – v.

Non-organic crops have no significant **effect** on health.

It is difficult for individual customers to **affect** the way businesses behave.

practice – n. / *practise* – v. (NB   practise needs a **s**ubject)

The **practice** of using ice to prevent organs from deteriorating is relatively old.

Before doctors start to **practise** medicine they must complete several years of training.

Appendix 4
Overview of common referencing styles

There are five different referencing systems which are commonly used, and below is a very brief overview of each style.

Institutions may have their own variations of common referencing styles, particularly in the way page numbers are indicated, how brackets are used, whether book/journal titles are underlined, italicised or put in bold, and whether the list of sources is called a Reference List or a Bibliography. Don't worry about such variations at first – your tutors will not expect you to get every detail of referencing correct first time. The key points to remember are:

- indicate clearly in your esssay (not just in your bibliography) whenever you have used a source;
- check which referencing system your tutor wants you to use – you will usually be given a detailed guide on how to reference your work;
- be consistent in the way you reference.

1   Harvard referencing style. This is an author/year system commonly used in several disciplines.

In-essay references
Collins (1994:2) states that 'good ethics is synonymous with good management'.

or

Collins (1994) states that 'good ethics is synonymous with good management' (p. 2).

List of References
Collins, J. W. (1994) 'Is business ethics an oxymoron?' *Business Horizons* Vol. 37 (5), pp. 1–8.

NB   The bibliography in the Harvard system differs from the list of references because it includes all sources read, including those not actually mentioned in the essay.

2   American Psychological Association (APA) referencing style. This is an author/year system, commonly used in the social sciences.

In-essay reference
Collins (1994) states that 'good ethics is synonymous with good manage-ment' (p. 2).

List of References
Collins, J. W. (1994) 'Is business ethics an oxymoron?' *Business Horizons* 37 (5), pp. 1–8.

3   Modern Language Association (MLA) referencing style. This is an author/page system commonly used in social sciences, humanities and liberal arts.

In-essay references
Collins states that 'good ethics is synonymous with good management' (Collins 2).

Works Cited
Collins, John W. (1994) 'Is business ethics an oxymoron?' <u>Business Horizons</u> 37 (5): 1–8.

4   Vancouver referencing style. This is a numeric system often used in the field of medicine.

In-essay references
Collins (1) states that 'good ethics is synonymous with good management' (p. 2).
or
Collins[1] states that 'good ethics is synonymous with good management' (p. 2).

References
1. Collins J. W. Is business ethics an oxymoron? Business Horizons 1994; 37 (5): pp. 1–8.

5   Chicago/Turabian referencing style. This is another common numeric system, similar to the Vancouver style but with some differences in the way references are given in the footnotes.

In-essay references
Collins[1] states that 'good ethics is synonymous with good management' (p. 2).

Footnotes
1. John W. Collins, 'Is business ethics an oxymoron?' *Business Horizons* (1994): 37 (5), pp. 1–8.

Appendix 5
Complete business ethics essay

**Outline what business ethics is and discuss whether it is important.
(1,500 words)**

The subject of business ethics has become increasingly important over the past few decades and now appears to be a prevalent factor in consumer choice. An illustration of this is the current number of publications in the UK which give consumers information on so-called ethical companies. The Ethical Company Organisation (2008), for example, lists businesses ranging from pet food producers and florists, to banks and stationery companies. The UK ethical market is valued at over 40 billion euros per year and there are currently over 2,000 books and 4 million web entries related to business ethics (Crane and Matten, 2007). This essay will first describe what business ethics is and secondly, will consider whether this concept really is important. It will argue that business ethics is indeed a major issue in both the study and practice of business.

There are numerous but similar definitions of business ethics given by academic experts. Shaw and Barry (2007) define business ethics as 'the study of what constitutes right and wrong (or good and bad) human conduct in a business context' (p. 25). Another definition describes business ethics as the 'principles and standards that guide behaviour in the world of business' (Ferrell and Fraedrich et al., 2002, p. 6). A growing number of companies also have their own descriptions of what they understand by ethical behaviour. Many companies list only the quality, naturalness and sustainability of their products as their underlying ethical message. One example of a company statement which also includes the human dimension is the following: 'we will operate our business with a strong commitment to the well being of our fellow humans and the preservation of the planet' (Body Shop International, Policy on donations, May 2006, p. 1).

When describing what business ethics is, it is essential to clarify that it is not synonymous with the law or with morals in general. Although the law overlaps with ethics, it usually only regulates the lowest level of acceptable behaviour (Crane and Matten, 2007). In fact, business ethics is mainly concerned with issues and areas of business conduct which are *not* specifically covered by the law and which are therefore vulnerable to exploitation and to what is viewed as immoral behaviour, even though it may be legal (ibid.). As for morality, Crane and Matten explain that although morals are a basic premise, ethics and ethical theory go a step further and focus on how morals can be applied to produce explicit standards and rules for particular contexts, of which business is only one. Business ethics, then, is the study and *application* of moral norms and legislation to produce guidelines of good behaviour in business.

Is business ethics, then, a valid area of study and is ethical behaviour actually important to businesses? In answer to the first part of this question, there are indeed good reasons why this area of study is necessary. First, the power of organisations is increasing both nationally and globally and Crane and Matten point out that the decisions businesspeople make can have huge implications and consequences, yet managers often have no specific training in ethics. Therefore, the study of business ethics is crucial in providing guidelines for making business decisions. Secondly, the study of business ethics is needed to inform legislators on issues such as the definition of corporate responsibility. It is clear that there is much unethical behaviour by companies: recent well-publicised examples include Enron, McDonald's, Shell, Pepsico and Nike, and the study of business ethics is therefore needed to help legal bodies and society in general assess the degree to which certain business behaviour is unethical.

There are diverse opinions as to whether ethics do have a valid place in a business. These views range from a definite 'no', i.e. that ethics does not and should not play a part in business, to a clear 'yes' and the argument that ethical behaviour should be a core value in any organisation. Opponents of the concept of ethics in business include those who claim that making a profit is the only responsibility a business has to society (Friedman, 1970, cited in Fisher and Lovell, 2003). Others such as Wolf (2008) share this view, and Prindl and Prodham (1994) suggest that 'Finance as practised in the professions and in industry is seen as a value-neutral positive discipline promoting efficiency without regard to the social consequences which follow from its products' (p. 3). Carr (1968) uses the analogy of a poker game to argue that a successful businessman needs to play by the rules of business in which 'bluffing' is an acceptable form of behaviour, and that these rules are distinct from personal or social values. He suggests that even if a manager claims that good ethical conduct is also good for business, s/he is not really making a choice to be ethical but is merely using ethical conduct as a profitable business strategy.

It is of course true that most businesses cannot succeed without being profitable. However, this does not necessarily exclude ethical behaviour and although Carr's view seems persuasive, there are two strong opposing arguments which are even more so. First, businesses are clearly not separate from society, but part of it. As stated above, the actions of businesses have consequences for the wider national and often global community and as international companies produce more, they use increasingly large amounts of the world's resources across the globe. Increasingly, various types of stakeholders expect businesses to behave well. This is exemplified by the fact that customers, governments and even the financial markets, now expect companies to publish reports on their greenhouse gas emission and energy performance. If businesses do not reach expected targets, their reputation and possibly also their financial investment prospects are likely to suffer (Esty, 2007). Moreover, businesses are linked to societies across the globe because people in developing countries are now often employed by first world businesses. Although perhaps some consumers are only interested in an ethical company for image and product quality, increasingly 'citizens of first world societies expect their corporations to display integrity in their international business dealings' (Svensson and Wood, 2008, p. 312). It is true that although businesses need to be *seen* as ethical, the assumption cannot be made that they really *are* behaving in an ethical manner and, as already pointed out, managers are perhaps making ethical decisions only as a form of strategy for profit. Nevertheless, such external pressures, including current and future legislation on aspects of corporate responsibility, do mean that businesses are being forced to act more ethically, whatever the personal motivation of managers. Clearly then, businesses are not isolated from society. Svensson and Wood (2008) show that the two are in fact mutually dependent and that both are responsible for the consequences and effects of the other as part of a constant two-way process. Their model importantly demonstrates that the ethical standards of society are also those of business. Carr's argument that business ethics are different and separate from the ethics of other social contexts does not seem to hold true.

Secondly, an even stronger argument for the view that good ethics in business do in fact exist, is that given by Collins (1994) and other prominent experts on the subject. This is that 'good ethics is synonymous with good management' (p. 2). Collins states that if managers only concern themselves with profit, they will in fact become 'dysfunctional'. This is because any business is made up of people: employees, customers and other stakeholders. He suggests that if businesses do not operate with a degree of trust, co-operation and consideration, they will in fact be putting constraints on profitability. This idea of the interdependence of any business organisation is also supported by Shaw and Barry (2007), Green (1994), Fritzsche (2005) and Svensson and Wood (2008).

To conclude, companies do not always behave ethically, or even lawfully. However, we live in a world of constantly improving access to business information, reliance on reputation and increasing legislation in areas such as working conditions and sustainability. These are very real elements of business practice, where ethical decisions and good conduct are expected and/or required. Moreover, the long-term success of a business arguably requires a level of sound ethical conduct both externally and internally. Business ethics, then, are central to organisations, and business ethics as a field of study and research is therefore vital in order to help business managers tackle the ethical dimensions of their job and to inform legislators, governments and society on how ethics should be applied in business contexts.

Bibliography

Carr, A. Z. (1968) 'Is business bluffing ethical?' *Harvard Business Review*, 46 (1), pp. 143–153.

Collins, J. W. (1994) 'Is business ethics an oxymoron?' *Business Horizons*, 37 (5), pp. 1–8.

Crane, A. and Matten, D. (2007) *Business Ethics* (2nd edn). New York: Oxford University Press.

Esty, D. C. (2007) 'What Stakeholders Demand'. *Harvard Business Review*, 85 (10), pp. 30–34.

Ethical Company Organisation. Available at: www.ethical-company-organisation.org/ (accessed: 5 January 2008).

Ferrel, O. C., Fraedrich, J. and Ferrell, L. (2002) *Business Ethics: Ethical Decision Making and Cases.* Boston: Houghton Mifflin.

Fisher, C. and Lovell, A. (2003) *Business Ethics and Values.* Harlow, Essex: Pearson Education.

Fritzsche, D. J. (2005) *Business Ethics: A Global and Managerial Perspective* (2nd edn). Boston: McGraw-Hill Irwin.

Green, R. M. (1994) *The Ethical Manager.* New York: Macmillan College Publishing.

Prindl, R. and Prodham, B. (eds) (1994) *The ACT Guide to Ethical Conflicts in Finance.* Oxford: Association of Corporate Treasurers.

Shaw, W. H. and Barry, V. (2007) *Moral Issues in Business* (10th edn). Boston, MA: Thompson Wadsworth.

Svensson, G. and Wood, G. (2008) 'A Model of Business Ethics'. *Journal of Business Ethics,* 77, pp. 303–322.

The Body Shop, *Policy on Donations,* p. 1.

Available at: www.thebodyshopinternational.com (accessed: 20 January 2008).

Wolf, M. (2000) 'Sleeping with the enemy'. *Financial Times,* 16 May, p. 21.

Appendix 6
Exercises for further practice

(a) Paraphrasing
Paraphrase the source extract below.

Source extract

> The National Radiological Protection Board said that more than 50 million mobile phones are used in the UK today, a number that has doubled since 2000. The mobile phone industry has contended that no research has shown that mobile phone use is hazardous to the health of the public.
>
> (Adapted from: Telecommunications Reports (2005) 'U.K. Finds "No Hard Evidence" of Cellphone Health Risk', 71 (2), pp. 19–20.)

(b) Summarising
Read and make notes on the informative source text below. From your notes, write a one-sentence summary and then a two-sentence summary. Each summary should include an in-essay reference and reference reminder phrase. Compare your summaries with the examples given.

Source text

Sport in the UK: the role of the DCMS

The Department for Culture, Media and Sport (DCMS) is responsible for delivering Government policy on sport, from supporting the performance and preparation of elite individual performers and teams to increasing sporting opportunities at all levels, but especially for the young, to encourage long-lasting participation.

DCMS recognizes that success in sport by UK representatives at the elite level, such as athletes at the Olympics or football teams in European competition, can enhance the reputation of the country and make large numbers of people feel proud. To that end, it provides funding where it will make a difference, such as through the Talented Athlete Scholarship Scheme, and political support where that is more suitable, such as to the Football Association's attempts to be awarded the right to host the 2018 FIFA World Cup in England.

DCMS also supports opportunities to participate in sport in schools and communities, regardless of the level of performance. Among DCMS' targets are that by 2008, 85% of 5–16-year-olds will be taking physical education and other school sports for a minimum of two hours per week, and that by 2010 all children will have the opportunity of at least four hours of weekly sport (DCMS 2008).

Widening participation will help to identify the next generation of potential elite performers at an early stage, but DCMS also has other less obvious goals in mind. They claim that continued participation in sport from an early age will lead to a more active population and that this will help to address the problem of increasing levels and frequency of obesity and so reduce the risk of coronary heart disease, stroke, type 2 diabetes and certain types of cancer. Clearly, the benefits of sport to the nation are not simply about medal tables and championships.

(Source: Martin, C. (2008) *Sport and the Nation*.)

(c) Editing

(i)   Below is a student paragraph which contains mistakes, is unclear and lacks punctuation. Rewrite the paragraph correctly and then compare your version with the example answer.

Although there is an increase in the ability of organ transplantation to cure diseases and enhance the quality and length of lives patients there are many religious and cultural issues that inhibit the donation of organs resulting as an obstacle in transplantation.

(ii)   Below are ten sentences which contain different types of errors. Correct each sentence.

1 Crick (1995) describes that some of the possible advantages and drawbacks of the technique.
2 Diabetics people are those who cannot produce their own insulin.
3 Constraints should be put in its place to control research in this area.
4 Genes from other species have been introduced in to the organisms.
5 Education has been raised to a relatively well standard.
6 Some of the reasons for why patients recover are unclear.
7 The improvement was due to increase in the dosage.
8 By the respondents, only 25% felt that the new legislation would be effective.
9 Some religious does not permit blood transfusions.
10 The most popular research carried out on gene modification is to produce larger amounts of food.

(iii)   The sentences below contain informal phrases. Rewrite them in a more formal style.

1 It all starts off in the lungs.
2 Can we get sick by using mobile phones?
3 When it comes down to it, there is no firm evidence for this theory.

4   This idea can be backed up by research studies.
5   If we do not find a solution the policy will fall apart.
6   Plant gene manipulation is a great way of increasing crop yield.

(d) Using words such as *however*, *although*, *nevertheless*, *in addition*

Write a paragraph that compares online sources with printed articles and books. Describe the similarities, differences, advantages and disadvantages of using these two source formats for essays. (There is no answer for this exercise but you may like to ask someone to read your paragraph and comment on your use of the linking words.)

Appendix 7
Answers to practice execises

● **Part A**

Section A1
Practice 1

1. Reliable information for general issues on disability but may be biased. Not an academic source.
2. Not reliable and not an academic source.
3. Reliable and an academic source but 2002 is quite old for such a topic, which decreases the reliability of the information.
4. a. Reliable for some ideas on issues but may be biased and inaccurate. Not an academic source.
   b. Reliable and an academic source.
   c. Quite reliable but not an academic source.
5. Reliable for introducing main issues but not an academic source. Also the booklet is quite old for this topic and this further decreases how reliable the source is for information on animal cloning.
6. Probably reliable as information from businesses but not an academic source. You would also need to check when the website was updated.
7. Not reliable and not an academic source.
8. Reliable as information from businesses but not an academic source.
9. Reliable for general discussion and ideas but not peer-reviewed and therefore not academically reliable. You should find and use articles from the centre's 'Journal of Ethics' for academic sources.
10. Not reliable and will be biased, as it seems to be written by a pressure group. Not an academic source.

Section A2
Practice 2

Questioning
Carr assumes that businessmen are ethical in their private lives – this may not be true. He also assumes that all businesses operate in the same way, that they all have ethical standards separate from private ones and that you always have to choose between losing and lying. This may not be true – there may be other options or other types of business models.

Evaluating

His style is quite persuasive – I instinctively feel he is partly right – but he is very cynical and oversimplifies. He gives no evidence for his views and doesn't try to be objective or look at opposing evidence. His argument isn't very well ordered as it is continuous opinion rather than a developed argument. I agree with Carr that some people feel they do need to lie in business but not that this is always the case or that business ethics are totally separate from social norms – particularly nowadays? I will use Carr as a key source to show an expert who opposes the idea of business ethics and I will then criticise his argument by giving opposing evidence from Svensson and Wood.

Locating

Carr's article seems to have been radical and important at the time (1968) because a lot of other texts still refer to it. In terms of business ethics he is definitely in the 'no' camp. His article is very dated now and things have moved on since then – now there is more legislation on regulation of corporate behaviour, corporate transparency and accountability and more emphasis on ethics and sustainability.

Section A3

Practice 3

Example notes

	Carr, A. Z. (1968) 'Is business bluffing ethical?' *Harvard Business Review*, 46 (1), pp. 143–153. Notes written on 16/2/2009
p. 145 main point.	Ethics of bus. are like the rules of poker (distrust) – diff. from 'civilised human relationships'.
p. 145 (bottom) Not true?	Most busmn. are ethical in private lives, but at work they stop being 'private citizens' + follow the *different*. ethical rules of bus.
p. 148	The image that bus. gives of using ethics from private life e.g.' "Sound ethics is good for business" ' is only a self-serving + profit making deception, not a true ethical position.
p.153 (Conclusion) Not true now/all businesses? – other choices?	'To be a winner, a man must play to win'. Busmn will sometimes have to choose betwn. losing and 'bluffing' (lying) like poker. To succeed he will have to 'bluff hard'.
2nd main point	'Bluffing' is 'integral' to business.

NB   'Sound ethics is good for business' is a quotation by Carr in the original text. The student has made this clear in his notes by using double and then also single quotation marks to show that Carr is quoting someone else.

Section A4

Practice 4

1   This quotation is not special in what it says or how it is expressed. The student should have given this information in their own words as far as possible, for example: *Kzanty (2004) states that organs such as the lungs, pancreas and heart are used in transplantation.*

2   This information is common fact and knowledge so can be given in the essay without attribution to the author.

3   The quotation partially contradicts the student's point that transplants save lives.

4   The quotation is about the student's first point (improvements in transplantation techniques using animal organs), not about the point that is immediately in front of the quotation, that patients do not have to wait for transplants.

5   The quotation is not introduced clearly – it does not explain which trial or study is referred to or who 'everyone' is.

Practice 5

1   There are no quotation marks and no in-essay reference. This is plagiarism.

2   There is an in-essay reference but no quotation marks. This is plagiarism.

3   There are quotation marks but no in-essay reference. This might be seen as plagiarism.

4   There are quotation marks and an in-essay reference, but the authors' names should not be in brackets and the page number is missing. The page number must be included for quotations if you use the author/year system of referencing.

Practice 6

1   The student has added the word 'business' to the original wording. She should either take this word out or put it in square brackets, e.g. [business].

2   The student has taken out the words 'synonymous with' from the original text. She should use . . . to show this, for example: *This is that 'good ethics is . . . good management' (p. 2).*

3   The topic words 'good ethics' are used twice, once in the introductory sentence and again in the quotation. They should be used in one or the other but not both, for example: *This is that good ethical behaviour 'is synonymous with good management' (p. 2)*, or *This is that 'good ethics is synonymous with good management' (p. 2).*

4   The full-stop at the end of the quotation is inside the quotation marks. It should come outside the quotation marks after the page number brackets, for example: *This is that 'good ethics is synonymous with good management' (p. 2).*

Correct version of the extract using a numeric system of referencing

Secondly, an even stronger argument for the view that good ethics in business do in fact exist, is that given by Collins and by other prominent experts on the subject. This is that 'good ethics is synonymous with good management' (1).

Works Cited

1. J. W. Collins. 'Is business ethics an oxymoron?' *Business Horizons* 1994; 37 (5): 1–8.

Section A5

Practice 7

1 The paraphrase itself is good as it is written in the student's own words. However, there are no in-essay references and so this counts as plagiarism.

2 The paraphrase is rewritten in the student's own words and has an initial in-essay reference. However, there is no reference reminder phrase in the second sentence and so it is not clear whether this sentence is an idea from the student or from the source. This could be seen as plagiarism.

3 There is only one in-essay reference, given at the end of the paragraph. It is therefore not clear whether the first sentence is the student's idea or an idea from the source – this could be seen as plagiarism. It is much better to integrate a reference into the first sentence of a paraphrase and then to use reference reminder phrases.

4 This paraphrase consists of one sentence copied from Cox and a second sentence copied from the Maier, Blakemore and Koivisto text. The sentences have been stitched together without the use of quotation marks and without adequate referencing. This is plagiarism.

Example of an acceptable paraphrase of the Cox extract

Using the author/year style of in-essay referencing:

> Cox (2003) suggests that advising caution in the use of mobile phones is an example of a typical approach to the fear of a possible health risk which may be of a serious nature. He states that such an approach may have negative consequences, but is taken because although there may in fact be no health risk, this has not yet been proven.

Using the numeric style of in-essay referencing:

> Cox (1) suggests that advising caution in the use of mobile phones is an example of a typical approach to the fear of a possible health risk which may be of a serious nature. He states that such an approach may have negative consequences, but is taken because although there may in fact be no health risk, this has not yet been proven.

> Works cited
> 1. D. R. Cox, 'Communication of risk: health hazards from mobile phones'. *Journal of the Royal Statistical Society: Series A (Statistics in Society)* 2003; 166 (2): 214–246.

Section A6

Practice 8

Example of a good personal reflection on the Robinson text

Robinson states that Côté and Morgan's study shows a strong link between regulating emotions at work and job satisfaction and intentions to quit.

Robinson doesn't go into great detail about the Côté and Morgan study, so I would need to read the original text to really do a critical analysis of it and find out whether the experiment has any flaws. However, just from reading Robinson's summary of the study, it seems to me to be an important experiment – the only one I have found so far on emotion regulation. I think that the idea of regulating emotions at work and the effects this has on how someone feels about their job is very interesting.

Thinking about the essay title, I think that Côté and Morgan's findings imply that if you have a personality that is good at regulating your emotions and particularly that if you are able to be (or at least pretend to be) positive, then you are likely to have a higher level of job satisfaction than someone who can't or doesn't want to amplify positive emotions.

The findings also show that if you suppress negative emotions, you will have less job satisfaction. I think that this shows that if you are someone who can express negative feelings in a constructive way at work in order to find a solution to the problem, then you will probably have more job satisfaction than someone who just always hides negative emotions without trying to do anything about them.

Practice 9 (see pages 44–46)

● **Part B**

Section B1

Example sentences for introducing your own point - content of the sources which would follow the sentences.

1 Evidence of the different viewpoints.
2 Evidence of these two different views.
3 Examples of misconceptions about cloning.
4 Examples of these different opinions.
5 Evidence that organic crops do not use fertilisers or pesticides.
6 Evidence of lower yields.
7 Evidence of this research.

Practice 10 (other alternatives are possible)
1 comprises, consists of, is composed of. These words are used when you state that the whole is comprised of parts of that whole. The word *constitutes* is used when you start with the parts and say that they constitute the whole.
2 discuss/outline/focus on, centre on, address, consider, my essay is concerned with
3 aspect of/consequence of/effect of (<u>concept</u> means 'idea')
4 in my view/opinion (NB   It would be better to use <u>I have shown that</u>)
5 aspects of/issues related to

6 issue/debate on/question of
7 includes
8 introduced
9 recent
10 issue/question – used for something that can be debated/argued for or against.
11 controversial (*debatable* means questionable/not true) perspective/viewpoint
12 widespread – means 'used/occurs in many different places'. *Thorough* is used for actions that are done with completeness.

Practice 11

Example paraphrase

Wheeler (1998) points out that sustainability is clearly <u>an important aspect of</u> urban planning. He states that taking a long-term <u>view</u> when planning is <u>fundamental </u>to sustainability, although in practice, long-term plans are not always <u>considered</u>.

Section B2

Practice 12

1 studying/examining/investigating the possible ...   *Undergo* is only used for the people or things to which the experiment or event happens. E.g. *The patient will undergo two operations. Undergo* is not used with *about*.
2 show/prove/illustrate.   It is already clear that cigarettes are harmful – the evidence is to show to what extent (how much) they damage health.
3 suggests/implies.   The word *impose* has a very different meaning.
4 states/suggests/shows (other verbs are also possible).   The verb *mention* is only used to refer to a minor point and therefore should not be used when summarising.
5 conceived.   This means when an idea is first thought of. *Perceived* means 'thought of/viewed' in a particular way.
6 invented.   *Establish* means 'to set up something that continues', e.g. a company, charity or theory. *Discovered* would also be incorrect, as this verb can only be used when something is first found that already existed.
7 conveyed.   This means 'communicated'. *Portrayed* means 'represented or described in a particular way'.
8 The student has used the wrong verb (*implied*) to introduce the quotation. The quote from Murtaz is a clear statement, not something which he has only implied but not openly said. The student could have used a verb such as *stated*, *argued* or *asserted*.
9 The verb *claim* is usually used to show that you do *not* agree with what the author says in the quotation. However, the student goes on to say that her essay will show that she thinks the statement in the quotation is correct. A more appropriate verb would have been a positive verb such as *show* or a neutral verb such as *state* or *suggest*.

10 discusses the portrayal . . .   The verbs *discuss, describe* and *define* in the active tense are not followed by a preposition (e.g. *about, in, at, on*). They are followed by a noun phrase only (e.g. *I will discuss the issue* or *Smith describes the effects*).

11 This essay will *argue that there is a link* between regulating emotions and job satisfaction.   The verbs *argue* and *conclude* can only be followed by *that* + subject verb phrase.

12 Emotion regulation is defined as hiding or trying to modify your emotions. Verbs such as *describe* and *define* used in the passive tense for definitions are followed by *as*, not *that*.

Section B3

Practice 13: Error correction

1 exacerbating/worsening   *Enhancing* means improving something neutral or positive.

2 Encourages/forces

3 worsened/exacerbated   To *exaggerate* means to pretend that something is better or worse than it really is.

4 highlights/emphasises

5 distinct/definite   *Certain* or *high* would also be incorrect.

6 sharply/steeply/quickly   You cannot say *highly rising* or *highly increasing*.

7 eliminated

8 implies   Evidence/data implies something and we *infer* things from the data or evidence.

9 implication

10 speculate   To *speculate* means to form a theory about something – it is often used for past events. To *predict* means to try to determine future events.

11 increase/enhance/improve   To *ameliorate* means to improve a negative situation or problem.

12 approximately   *Generally* means 'in most cases/most of the time'.

13 a rise   To discuss data, use the noun *a rise* meaning 'an increase' or the verb *to rise*. For example: Numbers have risen this year. Numbers rose last year.
    following   *Subsequent* is used to refer to all time after a certain point. *Following* can be used for a specific year or point.

Practice 14

Example summary
Since 1901, the annual birth rate has been greater than the number of deaths, and until the middle of the 1990s this natural change was the principal cause of the increase in population (UK Government National Statistics, 2008).

Section B4

Practice 15: Error correction

1 In addition, Moreover, Also, Furthermore, . . .   These phrases are used when

the ideas in the two sentences are either both positive or both negative. In the example, both of the sentences express negative aspects of organic crops.

2 diverse/wide   *Distinct* means 'different from something else'.

3 differentiate between/make a distinction between   *Contrast* is used without *between* to compare very different things in some detail.

4 However, In contrast, On the other hand, . . .

5 Not a complete sentence. *Although* needs one sentence with two full clauses. For example: Although parallel computing can calculate huge amounts of data, in many ways it is still unable to equal the human brain.

6 However, Still, Nevertheless,/. . . effective although they still . . .

7 nor

Practice 16

Example of an essay paragraph that compares the three theories
There are three <u>distinct</u> theories of job satisfaction. One model states that both job type and employee personality are central to determining job satisfaction. This is because organisational structure influences the characteristics of a job, and jobs with particular characteristics attract people with particular personality attributes. These attributes in turn affect how satisfied a person will be with their job (Oldham and Hackman, 1981). <u>In contrast</u> to this model, the dispositional approach sees a person's disposition (or personality) as the most important element in determining the level of job satisfaction, regardless of job type (Staw, Bell and Clausen, 1986). Finally, Locke's theory of job satisfaction <u>differs from</u> both of the above, as it regards what a person wants to do in a job and how far these goals are achieved, as the main factors which determine job satisfaction (Locke, 1968).

Section B5

Practice 17

Discussion of a source
Although Carr's argument may <u>seem</u> persuasive, <u>it has several flaws</u>. His <u>view lacks evidence</u> and he <u>does not take into account the fact that</u> business decisions are not always as clear cut as he suggests. He also <u>fails to consider</u> other potential business models and practices and <u>ignores the fact that</u> total separation of business from society is not possible.

Section B6

Practice 18: Error correction

Suggested answers (other alternatives are possible).

1 detrimental to/has negative effects on   (avoid using *good* and *bad*)

2 which should not be allowed to continue

3 resolved/solved/dealt with by

4 There is no evidence that . . .
5 The fundamental issue is whether you have the ability to regulate your emotions.
6 complex/difficult to understand
7 The most important/fundamental point is that . . .
8 isolated from society
9 If this (trend) continues
10 They were surprised/confused by the results.
11 Organ transplantation is not effective.
12 Patients should not be treated like this.
13 They should not be interfered with/disturbed.
14 It will not help us. Or: It will not solve the problem/situation.
15 This situation is very different.
16 . . . cannot continue
17 Globalisation is likely to have negative effects on the human species.
18 There are different kinds of businesses such as private, public and non-profit making.
19 It's a serious/significant problem.
20 action to take/step to take

Practice 19

Côté and Morgan demonstrated that as they predicted, the suppression of unpleasant emotions leads to a decrease in job satisfaction and therefore an increase in intention to quit. Their findings also suggest that an increase in the amplification of pleasant emotions will increase job satisfaction because it increases positive social interaction and more positive responses from colleagues and customers (Côté and Morgan, 2002, cited in Robinson, 2008).

 Part C

Section C1

Practice 20

Important or importance?

1	differentiates	v.
2	percent	n.
3	tourists	n.
4	advantages	n.
5	continues	v.
6	contribution	n.
7	clearly	adv.
8	religious beliefs	adj. + noun
9	confidentiality	n.
10	To conclude	v.

11 the risk to health   (NB   in lists, all parts of the list should follow the same
                            grammatical pattern, in this case a noun phrase.)
12 potential   adj.

Practice 21

Have or has?
1 has increased   (the number of + *has*)
2 report
3 shows
4 helps
5 has been   (malicious software + *has*)
6 differ
7 has
8 implies
9 has   (the use of + *has*)
10 Much research is
11 is reabsorbed
12 is the weight
13 Much/A great deal of information

Sentence structure

Practice 22

1 For example, the risk to the health of the patients **is** high.   (Sentence needs a
   verb.)
2 Firstly, I will **discuss** the positive aspects of drug therapy.   (Sentence needs a
   verb.)

Practice 23 (suggested answers)

3 Although there are several advantages, there are also drawbacks.
4 Our data, which shows a direct correlation between lack of light and depression, **is**
   flawed.

Practice 24

5 Dorkin argues that
6 Herschel points out that
7 Donne states that

Practice 25

8 Côté and Morgan have shown that emotion regulation influences job satisfaction
   and that amplifying positive emotions increases positive interaction with both

colleagues and customers. However, they have found that there is not an opposite correlation, that is, that job satisfaction affects emotion regulation.

9 The business decisions managers take can have significant implications **but/yet** most managers do not have training in business ethics.

or:

The business decisions managers take can have significant implications. However, most managers do not have training in business ethics.

10 The worldwide web is a constantly developing technology; it has many advantages for society.

or:

The worldwide web is a constantly developing technology **and** it has many advantages for society.

Practice 26

In, *at* or *on*?

1 cited in
2 effects on
3 I will discuss violence   (*discuss* is never followed by *about*)
4 broken down into
5 Prevention of
6 be drawn as to whether
7 They all contribute to making
8 in a constant state of balance
9 negative effects of
10 pertinent/relevant to the experiment
11 the similarities between
12 From an Islamic perspective

Practice 27

To find *or* finding?

1 capable of making
2 is caused by the cutting down
3 The process of utilising the waste
4 The failure of cells to remove
5 rejects the idea of using DNA

Practice 28

The *or* nothing?

1 among society
2 the public
3 the University of North Texas
4 in society

 5 the burning of coal
 6 The third disadvantage
 7 the UK
 8 the majority of people
 9 The author's position
10 the Amazon Basin
11 the immune system
12 The exam timetable . . . the exam

Practice 29

Commas with *that*
 1 It has been shown in this essay that this is not the case.
 2 It is illogical that people think pollution is not important.
 3 The fact is that we cannot determine the outcome.
 4 This essay will discuss the most important aspect of genetic research, that is, cloning.

Practice 30

Commas with *which*
 1 Many commentators have suggested that a system which (that) allows different states to have autonomy would be best.
 2 There are many factors which (that) may affect the way a text is written.
 3 Patel's data, which was collected from over 300 questionnaires, showed that our proposition was correct.
 4 The data which (that) was collected by the first research team proved not to be as reliable as the data collected in later studies.

Practice 31

Apostrophes
 1 theologists
 2 its
 3 A country's
 4 employee's
 5 whose
 6 body's
 7 experiments
 8 Its main proposition is that the women's movement in the 1960s to 1980s . . .
 9 Employees
10 The researchers' data

Practice 32

Direct and indirect questions
1 The question is whether mobile phones make us sick.
2 The issue is whether this will lead to an increase in violence.
3 Research was conducted to see what the cause of the disease was.
4 It is unclear what the key issue in global warming is.
5 The question remains as to what this research has achieved.

Section C2

Practice 33

In-essay references
1 According to Reynolds (2000) . . .
2 According to Padash (2000) . . .
3 Marchais (1984) discusses . . .
4 Locke (1997) suggests that . . .
5 Inadequate reference. The author (or organization if no author) and year should be given, as with any reference. Words such as *article* or *book* should never be used as part of a bracketed reference.
6 The author would be referred to as with any other reference, not the website. For example: McDermot (1999) has drawn attention to the fact that more research needs to be done.
7 You should not normally give the title of the book, and details such as edition numbers should not be used in an in-essay reference (in fact *Economics* is only part of the book title; if you do want to include the title it must be in full and accurate). The correct reference should be '(Sloman, 1997)'.
8 Inadequate reference. If you want to include the title of an article or book you must also give the author and year. For example: These factors are discussed by Smith (1990) in the article titled 'Biometric data of the future'.
9 The year must be included and there should not be quotation marks around the authors' names.
10 There is no in-essay reference.
11 Do not use bold, underlining, italics or any other type of font with in-essay references (italics are sometimes used for a book/article title).
12 The author and year should be used rather than the article title. If the article title is included it should use capitals on main words, with either italics or quotation marks.

Practice 34

Quote, cite, source
1 In my view, . . .   'According to' is only used with other people, e.g. According to Nitka (1980) . . .
2 Kerlinger (1969) states that

3   Jones (2002) demonstrates/shows that governments . . .   Don't mention details
such as a book having been written or published.
4   As Collins states/suggests/claims, . . .
5   These factors are discussed in the article 'Dying to be thin'. Author and year should
also be given.
6   The issue . . . is controversial.   Don't write about your reading/research
process unless asked to do so as a specific part of the assignment.

Practice 35

Sentence grammar
1   Côté and Morgan (1999) showed that . . .
2   Coates and Bailey (1995) examined . . .
3   According to the *New Scientist* (8/1/2005) people are still not . . .
4   As Crème and Lea (1997) have stated, the gap between . . .
5   According to Smith (2000) the problem is widespread.

Practice 36

Grammar and punctuation with quotation
1   It is unclear where the quotation ends as there are three quotation marks. There is
also an incorrect extra bracket at the end of the sentence.
2   Knowles (1998) states that 'groups work more efficiently' (p. 64).
NB   This information is not special enough to use as a quotation and should have
been paraphrased.
3   A reporting verb is needed to introduce the quotation. Also the information is not
special enough to quote. The year should be in brackets.

Section C3

Overgeneralisation, unspecific and unsupported statements

1   You cannot give statements such as this in academic writing, as they are opinion
and stereotype rather than proven or reasoned statements. The nearest statement
to this you could make would be if you were discussing specific characteristics or
abilities, supported by evidence. For example: 'In some respects, women seem to
have superior skills or attributes to men, such as . . . This is supported by Smith
(2000) who shows that . . .'
2–8 These statements may or may not be true but you would need to give details and
evidence to support them. Words such as *millions* are too vague. Never use the
words *everyone* or *no-one*, or *we all see*, as this is overgeneralisation. It would be
extremely unlikely (and not possible to prove) that everyone or no-one feels,
thinks or acts in the same way. Statements 2–6 also need a specific context, e.g.
worldwide or UK.

Not explaining yourself clearly

1 The pollution in the Mediterranean, which is the dirtiest sea in the world, is caused by tourism.
2 I have chosen to discuss cloning because I want to discuss the major advances in this technology and why cloning should be prohibited.
3 The issue of cloning animals, and possibly humans, has been debated by scientists, politicians and the general public.
4 The nephron has five main parts/components which are all essential for the process to work.
5 Academic writing is a form of writing that students need to adapt to and use in their work.
6 Personal writing is more concerned with personal feelings than with objective facts.
7 This is a development in the country's tourism industry.
8 *Vice versa* can only be used for a direct reversal of two things. In this sentence it would mean that deoxygenated blood is also pumped from the lungs into the heart. This is not correct, as only oxygenated blood is pumped back from lungs to heart.   NB   *Vice* is spelt with a *c* (it is not *visa versa*).
9 The use of the pronoun *they* means that the reader is not sure whether it is the children or the parents who behave aggressively. Also, the pronoun *them* could refer to films or to parents. If there is more than one subject in a sentence, use the full noun instead of a pronoun, or alter the sentence so that there is nothing in between the noun and the pronoun it refers to. For example:

> Luchens (2006) found that some children are allowed to watch violent films by their parents and that **the children** behave more aggressively after watching them.

or

> Luchens (2006) found that **some parents allow their children** to watch violent films and that **they** behave more aggressively after watching **them**.

Section C4
Alternative answers are possible for some sentences.

Missing words or phrases

1 When deforestation *occurs*, . . . and *it* cannot remove carbon dioxide.
2 A good dictionary is *used* to find . . .
3 'Cultural baggage' is *when* tourists *carry* their own values *with them*.
4 For example, *there **is** a* correlation between diet and disease.   (Sentence needs a verb.)
5 . . . the final stage which *takes place in* the second coiled tubule.

6 ... the rejection *of the organ by* the immune system.
7 ... morally wrong and *that it* should therefore be classified as illegal.
8 ... to be happier than you are, *you will increase job satisfaction.*
9 ... to search *for* each word that we do not know, *to gain* at least ...
10 *It* is clear that ...

Extra words or phrases

1 *Although* should be deleted, or a second clause added to the sentence.
2 *with* should be deleted.
3 *it* should be deleted.

Wrong phrase order

1 Whether animal testing is right or wrong has been disputed. (It would be better to write this as 'The rights and wrongs of animal testing have been debated.')
2 There is a natural connection between spoken language, for example the accent, vocabulary and discourse patterns, and the cultural identity of a group.

● **Answers to further practice exercises**

(a) Example of an acceptable paraphrase
Using the author/year style of in-essay referencing:

> According to the Telecommunications Reports (2005), the mobile phone indus-
> try states that there is no evidence to suggest phones damage the health of
> users, and that the number of phones in the UK in 2005 (50 million) had
> doubled in five years.

Using the numeric style of in-essay referencing:

> According to the Telecommunications Reports (1), the mobile phone industry
> states that there is no evidence to suggest phones damage the health of users
> and that the number of phones in the UK in 2005 (50 million) had doubled in
> five years.

> Works Cited
> Telecommunications Reports. 'U.K. Finds "No Hard Evidence" of Cellphone
> Health Risk'. 2005; 71 (2): 19–20.

(b) Example of a one-sentence summary of the Martin text
Martin (2008) describes how the UK Department of Culture, Media and Sport supports all levels of sport but particularly for children, with the aim of encouraging life-long physical activity and good health.

Example of a two-sentence summary of the Martin text
Martin (2008) describes the main aims of the UK Department of Culture, Media and Sport as not only funding and supporting sport of all types and at all levels, but in particular, of increasing the amount of sporting opportunity and activity of school-age children. Martin states that the DCMS hopes that its specific targets in this area will lead to an improvement in the long-term physical health of the UK population.

(c) Correction and editing

(i)   Although there has been an improvement in the ability of organ transplantation procedures to replace diseased organs and enhance the quality and length of patients' lives, there are religious and cultural issues that inhibit certain groups and individuals from donating organs. This results in fewer organs being available for transplantation.

(ii)   1   Crick (1995) describes some of . . .
       2   Diabetics are people who . . .
       3   Constraints should be put in place . . .
       4   . . . introduced into the organisms.
       5   . . . a relatively good/high standard.
       6   . . . reasons why patients . . .
       7   . . . due to an increase in . . .
       8   Of the respondents . . .
       9   Some religions do not . . .
     10   Most research carried out . . .

(iii) 1   The process starts/begins in the lungs.
       2   The question is whether the use of mobile phones damages health.
       3   There is no firm evidence for this theory.
       4   This idea is supported by research studies.
       5   The policy will fail if a solution is not found.
       6   Plant gene manipulation is a good/effective way of increasing crop yield.

Index